THE
COOK & THE
BUTCHER

# THE COOK & THE BUTCHER

## BRIGIT BINNS

photographs
**KATE SEARS**

weldon**owen**

# FOREWORD
## BY TOM MYLAN

Eight years ago, when I first moved to New York City, I was amazed to see all of the butcher shops in every neighborhood. Having grown up with big grocery stores with their displays of meat in plastic wrapped foam trays, I became obsessed with shopping at them. From the old Italian pork stores in the West Village where I worked at the time to the Polish butchers of Greenpoint where I lived, I'd pop in every other day to see what was new, what was good, to try something different, or buy a comfortable old favorite. Weekends found me and my girlfriend (now wife) browsing for pastured poultry at the farmer's market and staring in bewilderment at the cases full of offal in Chinatown.

After doing my shopping I'd hurry home to season, sear, bake, broil, braise, roast, or pan-fry my treasures from the shops and markets. Sure, I was a decent enough cook before I moved to Brooklyn but it was in that tiny galley kitchen on Clay Street where I started to learn how to really cook—and the butcher shops of New York were my muse. It was this passion and excitement about food in general and meat in particular that pushed me towards working in restaurants and, eventually, becoming a butcher myself.

There are few relationships more intertwined and essential to making good food than the collaboration between the cook and their butcher. Whether you're a home cook seeking an odd-ball cut for your great grandmother's recipe, a chef looking for a cooking technique for pig's feet, or just an average Joe trying to get inspiration for a Tuesday night dinner— your butcher is there to help.

That said, the give and take between you and your butcher is a relationship. Like all relationships, it helps to have loyalty, open-mindedness, and communication. In the beginning it's fine to date other butchers. But once you find that special one or two stay with them and shop with them regularly. You might be surprised how much more you can get out of a butcher who knows you as a regular.

Don't get me wrong; butchers certainly get a lot out of their customers as well. Our regulars have turned us on to cuts we didn't know existed, introduced us to new recipes, and brought us bundles of sausages we'd never heard of. From Shabu Shabu to Secreto, the people who come through the Meat Hook every day make our lives more interesting. They not only make us better at what we do but help shape how our shop evolves and changes to better serve our clientele. I hope that you get as much out of your butcher shops as I do out of mine. Not everyone who gets fired up by their trips to the butcher shop will go on to become a butcher, but you never know. At the very least, you'll become a better cook.

# A NOTE FROM THE COOK

I've been on a mission to master meat cookery ever since I served a raw standing rib roast to my new British in-laws. That dinner happened long before I authored my first cookbook, and it played a big role in my decision to both learn about and write about food. I never wanted anything like that to happen again.

Through the years, I have been fortunate to work with some wonderful butchers and chefs who have shared with me some of their secrets for preparing and cooking meat. In this book, I've adapted those lessons and incorporated them into the recipes so that the home cook can benefit from some flavor-boosting tricks of the trade while making everyday meals. Most of their techniques are surprisingly simple, such as letting meat come to room temperature and seasoning it generously before cooking, and roasting low and slow to ensure maximum tenderness and flavor. But one of the most important lessons I've learned from the pros is also the simplest: rely on a meat thermometer rather than a timer to judge when meat is perfectly cooked.

As you'll see in these pages, my approach is and always will be that of a home cook. Because when I'm done working, I like to cook. Meat. In my home kitchen. Which is just like yours. I hope you will enjoy using this collection of my favorite meat recipes to prepare memorable meat dishes for your own dinner table.

*Bridget L. Brines*

# ABOUT MEAT

It's a great time to be a meat eater. These days, you can purchase top-quality meat from a variety of sources—sometimes even directly from the farm or ranch where the animals were raised. You can even find out about the diets and living conditions of the animals, facts that make for easier shopping and smarter choices.

Nowadays, like many home cooks, I serve meat only a few times a week. That's primarily because the meat I purchase is better quality and costs more than what is typically available at the supermarket and, like many people, I need to watch my budget. I also cook smaller portions than I used to in years past, and then round out my menus with a salad, a complementary grain dish, and/or steamed or roasted vegetables. A bumper crop of labels has begun to appear on meats, often providing more confusion than clarity. So when I shop, I rely less on labels and more on my ability to identify good meat (see page 11). I also try to buy locally raised meat and heritage breeds whenever possible. If your butcher stocks meat from local producers, he or she will probably be able to tell you how it was raised, information that is usually more valuable than that on any label.

## MAKING THE CASE FOR FAT

In the late 1980s, when Americans were beginning to look for ways to cut the fat in their diet, the National Pork Board launched its "other white meat" campaign, which promoted pork as a lean, healthful meat. Pig farmers were already on board, selectively breeding their stock to remove as much naturally occurring marbling (intramuscular fat) as possible. The result was—and continues to be—pork with little taste and mediocre texture. That's because fat in any kind of meat equals good flavor and texture.

An external layer of fat on a standing rib roast or a leg of lamb helps meat remain juicy in the high, dry heat of an oven. At the same time, marbling lubricates from within, keeping meat succulent, tender, and flavorful. Some of the fattier cuts, such as pork or lamb shoulder, typically require slow, moist cooking to become tender. Others, such as a well-marbled T-bone steak, cook in just minutes. In all cases, the fat, both external and internal, acts as an efficient vehicle for flavor and texture.

This is not to dismiss the dangers of a high-fat diet. But more often than not, the culprits are deep-fried foods, fat-rich commercial snack foods, sweets, and the like, not a grilled lamb chop or a panfried beefsteak.

But labels can offer some clues about the meat, so understanding the most common terms found in stores is helpful. The two most ubiquitous terms are "certified organic" and "natural," both of which are regulated by the United States Department of Agriculture (USDA). Meat labeled "natural" has been minimally processed, with no artificial flavors, colors, or preservatives used in its production. Meat labeled "certified organic" further stipulates that the animals were raised on feed that was 100 percent organically grown and that they were administered no antibiotics or hormones during their lifetime. But these terms have their limitations, because they don't necessarily ensure that the animal was raised humanely. Currently, "certified organic" only requires that animals have "access to"—a phrase open to interpretation—the outdoors. Regulations may become stricter in the future, requiring that animals spend more time grazing on pasture, but the best way to ascertain that animals had a happy and comfortable life is to buy from a rancher or farmer with reputable practices.

Other frequently encountered terms on meat labels are "grass fed," used to describe animals raised on a diet of grasses, "free range," used for animals that are given "access to" the outdoors, and "pastured," used for animals that grazed freely. Meat from grass-fed and pastured animals is typically lower in fat and calories and higher in omega-3 fatty acids than meat from grain-fed animals, qualities that appeal to many shoppers.

Whether you buy responsibly raised local meat, or natural or organic meat from distant sources, you will pay more—in some cases, a lot more. But I believe that the opportunity to vote with your wallet on issues that affect your family's health, and the health of our planet, is worth every extra penny.

## SOURCING AND BUYING MEAT

For a while, butchers seemed to be going the way of phone operators. Rarely did you find anyone on hand to help you decipher the contents of those Styrofoam packages in the meat section of your local supermarket. Simply put, if you wanted to know whether to grill a flank steak medium-rare or the best way to cook short ribs, you were on your own.

But the situation has improved dramatically. Now, you have a steadily growing list of options on where you can purchase top-notch meat from knowledgeable, helpful people. Even the supermarket counter has more choices in terms of both quality and cuts, and more "service butchers," who will special order cuts, offer advice on which cuts are best for which cooking methods, and trim, tie, and even stuff meats. This means all you have to do is put your purchase in a pan on the stove top or in the oven.

I encourage you to seek out a high-quality butcher shop or supermarket meat counter and get to know the butchers who work there. If you live near a ranch that raises animals for meat or you frequent a farmer's market that includes meat vendors, you'll be able to buy directly from the people who raised and fed the animals. That immediacy has become more and more important as questions continue to arise on the ethics and safety of large-scale animal husbandry.

Whether you are buying meat from a cold case in a butcher shop or in the meat department of a grocery store, from a cooler in the back of a van at a farmer's market, or even in a Styrofoam package, you'll want to be able to recognize good meat. First, check the color: Beef should be cherry red to purplish red, not bright pink or brown. Lamb should be light red, and pork and veal should be rosy pink. The surface of any meat should be moist, not dry, and it should never be slimy or have a greenish iridescent cast, both of which signal spoilage. If you have any doubt at all about the freshness of a cut, let your nose be your guide (unless it is vacuum-packed). Don't hesitate to ask the butcher if you can smell the meat. If there is an off smell, choose another cut. Also, be sure to let the butcher know if his or her meat didn't pass your test. Nowadays, most butchers are proud of the meat they sell, and they want to know when it falls short of the best. Look for more information on buying specific cuts of meat on pages 18, 80, 142, and 188.

If you are buying packaged meat, check for the sell-by date. Packaged beef will occasionally include the USDA grade as well. See page 18 for information on the best grades to buy. Grades for pork, lamb, or veal are rarely included on packaging.

## LOCALLY SOURCED MEAT

Today, home cooks are more interested than ever in buying food that has been raised near where they live. For some time, they have been purchasing fresh fruits and vegetables at nearby farm stands and farmer's markets. Only now are they discovering that they can also buy locally raised meats.

BUYING A WHOLE ANIMAL  You may only do it once a year, but choosing an animal, having it slaughtered and butchered to suit your cooking preferences, and then dividing it among friends is an economical way to buy meat. Do some research to find a farm in your area that raises animals sustainably and humanely. You may even be able to visit the farm before making a commitment.

COMMUNITY-SUPPORTED AGRICULTURE (CSA) This program is a good way to source everything from fruits and vegetables to dairy products and meats and to support local farmers at the same time. Just as you can buy shares in a CSA that are paid out in a weekly box of fruits and vegetables, you can sign up with a meat CSA to receive boxes filled with assorted cuts. You will be helping the farmer by providing money in advance that can be used to purchase feed or other animal-related farm needs, and you will be receiving quality food at a better price because the middleman has been eliminated.

You may need to do some homework to find the right meat CSA for you, especially if you live in a city. You may also need to be patient, as the most popular CSAs often have waiting lists. Keep in mind, too, that availability, not your preference, will drive the contents of the box. That means that each delivery is likely to include a few different kinds of steaks and/or chops, a roast or two, and some cuts for stewing or braising.

## GAUGING MEAT DONENESS

THE TOUCH TEST  When heat begins to affect tissues, they start to shrink, shorten, and toughen. That means the more thoroughly cooked a piece of meat is, the springier it becomes. Poke a piece of meat with your index finger. If it is raw, it will feel quite soft and the surface will remain depressed. Rare meat will still feel soft but will be a little bouncy. Medium-rare meat will be a bit bouncier, and medium meat will be quite springy to the touch. With practice, this touch test will give you a good idea of the meat's doneness, but for accuracy, you will still want to test for doneness with a digital instant-read thermometer (dial face thermometers are not dependable).

DONENESS TEMPERATURES  In each chapter, you'll find a list of temperatures to help you identify when meat is ready to be removed from the heat, and the desired final temperatures of the meat after resting. While resting, the temperature of the meat will continue to rise 5° to 10°F (3° to 6°C), depending on the size and/or thickness of the cut and how long the meat is left to rest before serving. For example, rare beef is ready to be removed from the heat at 115° to 125°F (46° to 52°C), but then it rises to 125° to 130°F (52° to 54°C) after resting. I prefer to serve burgers medium (140° to 145°F/ 60° to 63°C), but if you have *any* question about the quality of the ground meat, cook to 160°F (71°C) for safety.

## COOKING METHODS

In the past, meat was usually cooked directly over an open fire or braised. These days, because we know more about how different cuts respond to different cooking methods and because we have more sophisticated tools for judging doneness, we can choose from a wider range of methods. When selecting your cut and your cooking method, always keep two principles in mind: First, opt for meat on the bone for the most flavor. Second, the amount of marbling will determine whether meat is best suited to high, dry heat or to moist, low heat.

PANFRYING, SAUTÉING, AND STIR-FRYING  Thin cuts of meat with minimal marbling are ideally cooked in a little fat over medium-high or high heat on the stove top. Cuts more than 1 inch (2.5 cm) thick will benefit from a pan-to-oven progression that mimics the high heat–low heat roasting described below: the meat is seared over high heat on the stove top and then finished in a moderate oven.

GRILLING  The ultimate high, dry-heat method, grilling imparts flavor, a nice crust, and a delicious smokiness to cuts as diverse as filet mignon and leg of lamb. Choose indirect-heat grilling for larger cuts and direct-heat grilling for steaks, chops, and kebabs. Be sure to baste or marinate leaner cuts, like flank steak, to ensure the fierce heat of the fire doesn't dry them out.

ROASTING  Large, well-marbled cuts are typically ideal candidates for roasting. In some instances, such as when cooking a beef tenderloin or other relatively small cut, only high heat is used. Otherwise, most cuts fare best when they are started in a very hot oven and then finished at a lower temperature. This ensures the meat will cook through to the center without toughening or overcooking.

RESIDUAL HEAT ROASTING  Once heat begins its journey from the outside of a piece of meat toward its center, it builds up momentum. If the oven is then turned off, the heat will continue to penetrate gently at an increasingly slower rate. This method of cooking in the oven's residual heat yields particularly juicy results. A probe thermometer is the best way to test proper doneness.

BRAISING AND STEWING  Both of these moist-cooking methods make worthy use of the tougher, less expensive cuts, such as shoulder, chuck, and shank, that contain lots of tasty collagen (connective tissue) but would toughen if exposed to the high, dry heat of roasting, grilling, or frying. You can also easily introduce flavor in both methods, with the addition of aromatic vegetables, spices, stocks, and wine.

The importance of cross-grain cutting when working with meat that has stringy muscle fibers—like tri-tip, flank steak, and skirt steak—cannot be stressed enough. Use your sharpest knife to cut perpendicularly through the fibers.

— Robert Fleming, Alexander's Prime Meats and Catering, San Gabriel, CA

# BEEF

# BEEF PRIMER

## BEEF AT A GLANCE

**Look for** slightly moist meat; light cherry red to brownish red color; marbled interior fat and white external fat; smooth, tight grain; clean, fresh smell.

**Avoid** sticky or wet meat; very deep purple meat; dark splotches; yellow fat with browning or darkening; stale or sour odors.

**Cuts to remember** tri-tip, skirt steak, hanger steak.

**Best value** chuck steak, shank, brisket, ribs.

**Splurge cuts** filet mignon, standing rib roast, top loin roast.

**Storage** 3 days in the refrigerator; up to 6 months in the freezer.

## BEST FLAVORS FOR BEEF

**American flavors** blue cheese, bourbon, horseradish, mustard, mushrooms, watercress.

**Asian flavors** garlic, ginger, soy, fish sauce, chiles.

**Mediterranean flavors** rosemary, peppercorns, Parmesan, wine, balsamic vinegar, leeks, fennel, arugula, tomatoes, olives, oregano.

**Latin flavors** lime, chipotle, cilantro, tequila.

Nowadays, good-quality beef is available from many sources. Grocery stores offer a wider selection than in the past, and the upsurge in gourmet food stores, neighborhood butcher shops, and farmers' markets has expanded the availability of grass-fed and other specially raised beef and hard-to-find cuts. You can make the best choices if you learn how to identify high-quality beef, and learn which cuts are best suited to particular cooking methods.

## BEEF GRADES

Grading beef is voluntary, and the United States Department of Agriculture (USDA) assigns grades to beef only if requested. Although the USDA uses eight grades, you are likely to see only three in stores: prime, choice, and select. The labels reflect specific characteristics: degree of marbling (the ratio of fat to lean meat), color, and maturity. Prime beef, the highest grade, is from young cattle and contains the most marbling. Choice beef lacks the degree of marbling found in prime but still produces a number of tender and juicy cuts. Select is a label applied to meat that is particularly lean. Select cuts are best when marinated or braised to enhance their flavor. The higher the grade, the more expensive the cut. Knowing the USDA grades is helpful, but you will also want to learn what qualities to look for so that you can assess any cut of beef on your own.

## GRAIN FED VS. GRASS FED

Grain-fed beef produces richly flavored meat with abundant marbling. The drawback is that the animals often live in close quarters in feedlots and require antibiotics to remain healthy. Consumers as well as chefs have rediscovered the taste and benefits of beef from cattle raised on grass. Some ranchers follow a hybrid process: the cattle feed on grass, which is healthier for them and better for the environment, and then, right before they go to market, they are "finished" on grain, which adds the rich marbling and tenderness of grain-fed beef. Experiment by trying cuts of beef from all three raising methods and decide which type you prefer.

## WET AGED VS. DRY AGED

Aging greatly improves the texture and flavor of beef, yielding a buttery character and intense taste. Most steaks have been wet aged, a process that involves sealing the meat in a vacuum-packed bag and refrigerating it from 1 to 4 weeks. Purists say that wet aging does little more than conserve moisture and does nothing to develop flavor. Dry-aged beef, which is stored unwrapped at a precise temperature and humidity level for several weeks, loses a large amount of moisture, which concentrates the flavor. It is expensive and makes up only 10 percent of the beef on the retail market. You might try a dry-aged steak and decide for yourself if the price is worth the difference in taste. Some cooks think the splurge is merited for simple preparations where the flavor of the beef shines through.

## BEEF BASICS

**TRIMMING** Most beef cuts have already been trimmed of fat before they are sold. As many recipes in this book instruct, you want to remove any sinew and excess pockets of fat on the surface prior to cooking. Some cuts, especially large roasts, may still have a layer of fat. Leaving about ¼ inch (6 mm) of fat on the surface helps baste the meat while it cooks, keeping it juicy. You can always ask the butcher to remove silverskin from a tenderloin or otherwise prepare a cut for a recipe you are making.

**BRINGING TO ROOM TEMPERATURE** The cooking times for the recipes in this book are based on room-temperature meat. The length of time required depends on the cut. A thin steak may be ready after 30 minutes, but a standing rib roast may take 3 hours. Meat not brought to room temperature, especially a large roast, will take longer to cook, and the surface of the meat will cook far more quickly than the interior.

**SEASONING** How to season your meat depends on the cut and cooking method. A high-quality steak destined for grilling needs a generous sprinkling of salt and pepper. Other cuts benefit from additional seasoning, in the form of a rub, paste, or marinade. If you marinate beef before cooking it with dry heat, be sure to pat the surface dry. Moisture on the meat will prevent it from browning and may even cause it to steam in the pan.

**RESTING** Allowing beef to rest after cooking—from 4 or 5 minutes for a steak to up to 2 hours for a large roast—is crucial to ensure properly cooked and juicy meat. During this resting period, the juices redistribute, and the meat finishes cooking, reaching its ideal doneness temperature.

**STORING** Store beef in butcher paper in your refrigerator. The ideal storage temperature for beef, 28° to 32°F (-2° to 0°C), is colder than most home refrigerators. You can use a thermometer to determine the coldest part of your refrigerator and store the meat there. Use refrigerated meat within 3 days, or freeze for up to 6 months. Large cuts freeze much better than smaller cuts, which dry out easily. The more marbled the beef, the better it will survive freezing: a chuck roast, for instance, will remain juicier than a tenderloin. Thaw meat slowly in the refrigerator; this may take 3 to 4 days for large cuts. Thawing meat in the microwave is not recommended, as the surface will begin to cook while the center will remain frozen.

## FAQS FOR THE BUTCHER

**Q: Should I buy individual steaks or a large one to share?**

**A:** For boneless steaks, like filet mignon or flat iron, I recommend individual portions. If you're cooking a bone-in cut, like a porterhouse, one large steak not only is more majestic but allows for a larger margin of error in the cooking time.

**Q: I'm on a budget. What are the most economical cuts?**

**A:** Braising cuts like beef shank (also called beef shin) and bottom round are great choices. One large piece of shank can be turned into a hearty ragout or barbecued beef sandwiches for four or five people.

**Q: I see meat labeled "100% Black Angus" in my market. Is this better than other beef breeds?**

**A:** Black Angus (also called Aberdeen Angus) is one of the first breeds to be selected and bred exclusively for making great tasting beef. In the U.S., it is the dominant pure bred beef cattle, although there are many others like Hereford and Short Horn that produce high-quality, tender beef.

—Tom Mylan, The Meat Hook, Brooklyn, NY

## COOKING BY THE CUT

**Best for stir-frying** tri-tip, top sirloin, and flank steaks; filet mignon.

**Best for panfrying** rib-eye, New York strip, T-bone, and porterhouse steaks; chuck (burgers).

**Best for grilling** rib-eye, skirt, sirloin, and strip steaks; chuck (burgers, kebabs).

**Best for roasting** stuffed flank steak; bone-in rib eye (standing rib roast); whole tenderloin.

**Best for braising** short ribs, brisket, shank, and chuck.

## TAKE THE TEMPERATURE

The lower temperatures in each range apply to roasts, the higher temperatures to steaks. (Roasts are removed from the heat at a lower temperature because the temperature rises more during a longer resting period.) Cooking beef until well done is not recommended.

**Very rare** remove from heat at 110°–120°F (43°–49°C); ideal temperature after resting: 120°–125°F (49°–52°C).

**Rare** remove from heat at 115°–125°F (46°–52°C); ideal temperature after resting: 125°–130°F (52°–54°C).

**Medium-rare** remove from heat at 125°–135°F (52°–57°C); ideal temperature after resting: 130°–140°F (54°–60°C).

**Medium** remove from heat at 130°–140°F (54°–60°C); ideal temperature after resting: 145°F (63°C).

**Medium-well** remove from heat at 145°–160°F (63°–71°C); ideal temperature after resting: 155°–160°F (68°–71°C).

## THE CUTS

Butchers first divide the animal into large sections, called primal cuts, as shown in the chart at right and listed below, and then divide the sections into retail cuts. In general, the tenderness of the meat is determined by the activity level of the muscles. The hardworking legs and shoulder sections, for instance, are tougher than the ribs and loin.

**CHUCK** Possessing a generous amount of fat and collagen (connective tissue), chuck is best suited to slow, moist cooking methods, such as braising and roasting, which render the meat lusciously tender and succulent. The chuck is also often ground for making burgers. There are two cuts from the chuck that are tender and lean: chuck eye and flat iron steak. Both cuts respond beautifully to brief grilling or pan searing.

**RIB** The generously marbled meat from this primal cut has a full-bodied flavor. Smaller cuts such as rib-eye steak and rib steak are ideal candidates for grilling and panfrying, whereas large cuts such as standing rib roast (the undisputed king of all roasts) are better for roasting. Slabs of meaty short ribs, cut between the ribs or across the ribs, respond best to braising.

**SHORT LOIN** Some of the most popular steaks come from this region: the porterhouse, consisting of a T-shaped bone between a strip steak and a juicy piece of the tenderloin; the T-bone, a smaller version of the porterhouse; and the strip steak, cut from the porterhouse The center section of the tenderloin is the source of the highly prized filet mignon.

**SIRLOIN** Just behind the short loin, this harder-working region yields tri-tip (also called culotte) and sirloin steaks. Sirloin steaks are chewier than steaks from the short loin, but are a good value. They are sometimes labeled according to the bone they contain: flat, round, wedge, or pin.

**ROUND** The meat in the leg region has minimal marbling. Many chefs consign the quite inexpensive round to making burgers or sausages. The lack of marbling is also plus when the meat is eaten cold, such as in a cold beef salad. Also, when cuts from the round are cooked using slow and gentle methods, the meat can be tender and tasty.

**FLANK AND PLATE** Running along the underside of the animal, the flank and plate produce the lean flank steak, skirt steak, and hanger steak, which benefit from marinating, and are delicious quick-seared or grilled.

**BRISKET** This tough cut gains flavor by long, slow cooking in aromatic liquid (braising) or by slow smoking. The brisket is also delicious when cured, as for pastrami and corned beef.

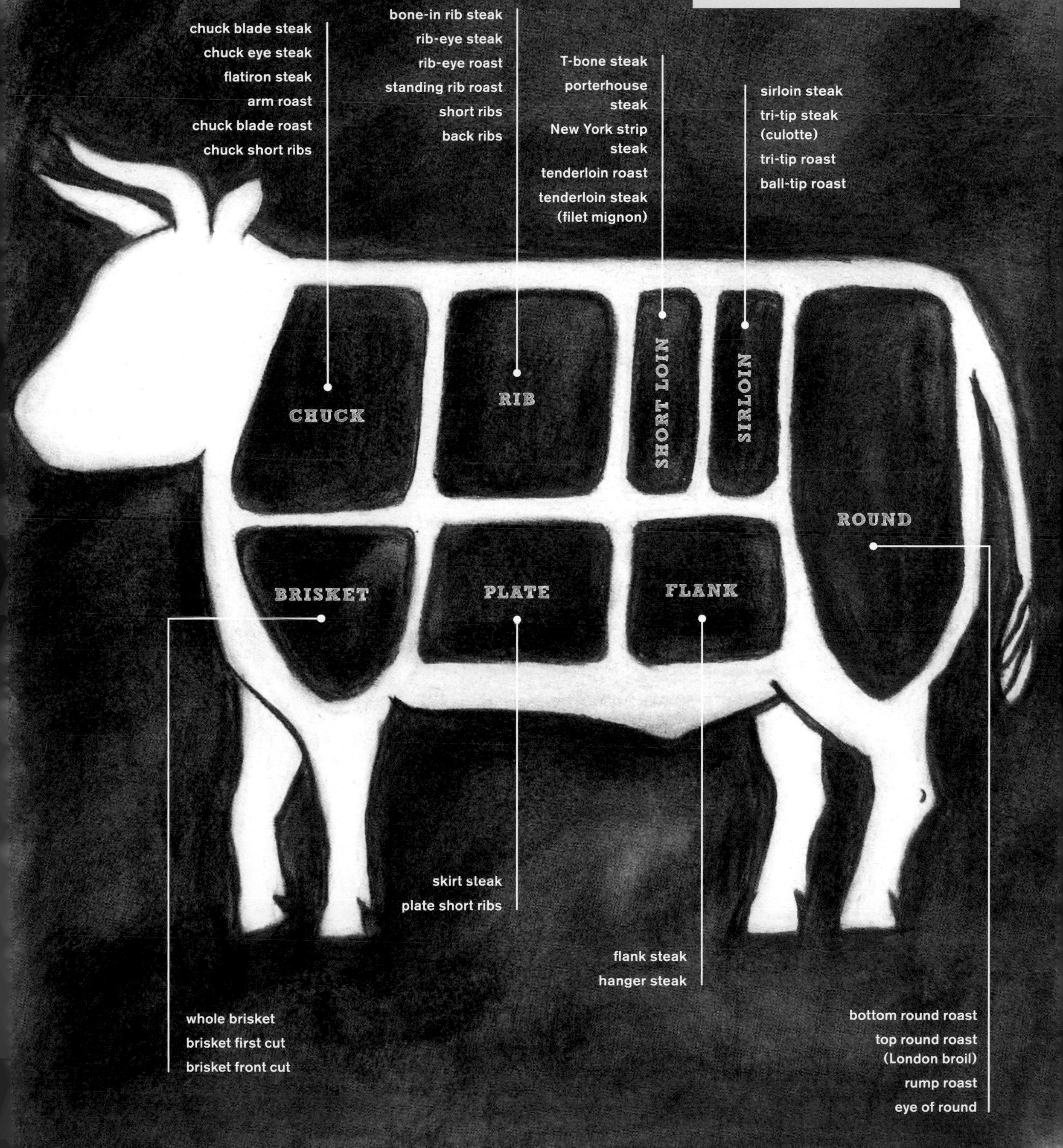

chuck blade steak
chuck eye steak
flatiron steak
arm roast
chuck blade roast
chuck short ribs

bone-in rib steak
rib-eye steak
rib-eye roast
standing rib roast
short ribs
back ribs

T-bone steak
porterhouse
steak
New York strip
steak
tenderloin roast
tenderloin steak
(filet mignon)

sirloin steak
tri-tip steak
(culotte)
tri-tip roast
ball-tip roast

CHUCK

RIB

SHORT LOIN

SIRLOIN

ROUND

BRISKET

PLATE

FLANK

skirt steak
plate short ribs

flank steak
hanger steak

whole brisket
brisket first cut
brisket front cut

bottom round roast
top round roast
(London broil)
rump roast
eye of round

## CARAMELIZED BEEF WITH ONIONS AND WATERCRESS

 MAKES 4–6 SERVINGS

Vietnamese flavors—fish sauce, rice vinegar, and garlic—marry with tender filet mignon in this recipe inspired by one of my favorite dishes served at the Slanted Door restaurant in San Francisco. Once you add the meat to the pan, don't move it for at least 2 minutes, or you will sacrifice a beautiful caramelized surface—the signature feature of this simple preparation.

In a resealable plastic bag, combine the garlic, white onion, fish sauce, sugar, ¾ teaspoon salt, a generous grinding of pepper, and 2 tablespoons of the oil. Add the beef, squeeze out some of the air, seal the bag, and turn to distribute the ingredients. Let stand at room temperature or in the refrigerator for 1½–2 hours. If the beef is refrigerated, return it to room temperature before cooking.

In a small bowl, toss the red onion with the vinegar and plenty of pepper. Let stand for 10–15 minutes. Add 1 tablespoon of the oil and toss. Divide the watercress and green onions among plates and arrange some of the red onion on top.

Remove the beef from the bag and discard the marinade. Place a wok or large, heavy frying pan over high heat, add the remaining 1 tablespoon oil, and swirl to coat the pan. When the oil has just begun to shimmer, add the beef, distributing it evenly, and cook without moving it until golden brown, about 2 minutes. Turn, add the butter, and cook for about 1 minute more. Do not overcook.

Arrange the beef and pan juices alongside the watercress. Serve at once.

6 cloves garlic, minced

½ small white onion, finely chopped

1 tablespoon Thai or Vietnamese fish sauce

1 teaspoon sugar

Kosher salt and freshly ground pepper

4 tablespoons (2 fl oz/60 ml) canola oil

1½ lb (750 g) filet mignon, cut into 1-inch (2.5-cm) cubes

1 small red onion, very thinly sliced

2 tablespoons rice vinegar

About 6 oz (185 g) watercress, tough stems removed

4 green onions, white and light green parts, finely chopped

1 tablespoon unsalted butter

---

 **A NOTE FROM THE BUTCHER**

For this recipe, use the center-cut piece of the tenderloin, called the filet mignon. The tail would be too stringy, and the tip end of the butt side has a small piece of gristle. Purchase the filet mignon from your butcher or buy a whole tenderloin and make the cut yourself. Make sure to cut off the membrane encasing the meat, called the silverskin, and remove the fat from the filet to ensure a clean piece for stir-frying.

—Jim Cascone, Huntington Meats, Los Angeles, CA

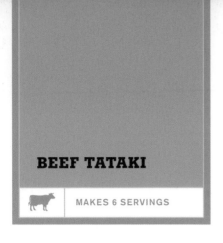

# BEEF TATAKI

🐄 MAKES 6 SERVINGS

This variation on classic beef carpaccio cooks the meat following a Japanese technique, *tataki*, that calls for quickly searing it over high heat so that the inside remains rare. Here, beef tenderloin is roasted at a high oven temperature, allowed to cool, and then flavored with a ginger-infused marinade. Generous slices of the beef are served drizzled with a bracing lemony sauce.

1 very cold beef tenderloin, about 2 lb (1 kg), silverskin removed

1 tablespoon canola oil

1 tablespoon sweet soy sauce (optional)

Freshly ground pepper

### FOR THE MARINADE

⅓ cup (3 fl oz/80 ml) reduced-sodium soy sauce

¼ cup (2 fl oz/60 ml) mirin or medium-dry sherry

1 tablespoon peeled and grated fresh ginger

3 green onions, white and light green parts, thinly sliced, plus slivered green onions for garnish

2 large cloves garlic, thinly sliced

Zest of 1 lemon, removed in strips with a vegetable peeler

### FOR THE CITRUS SAUCE

¼ cup (2 fl oz/60 ml) reduced-sodium soy sauce

2 tablespoons rice vinegar

1½ tablespoons turbinado or firmly packed dark brown sugar

2 tablespoons fresh lemon juice

2 tablespoons finely snipped fresh chives

Preheat the oven to 500°F (260°C).

Rub all sides of the beef with the oil, then rub it with the sweet soy sauce, if using. Season generously all over with pepper. Set on a rack in a roasting pan, place in the oven, and cook until an instant-read thermometer inserted into the tenderloin registers 115°F (46°C), 20–25 minutes. Immediately transfer the rack and beef to a rimmed baking sheet to catch the juices. Set in a cool place to stop the cooking as quickly as possible.

While the beef is cooling, make the marinade: In a large resealable plastic bag, combine the soy sauce, mirin, ginger, green onions, garlic, and lemon zest. When the beef is cool enough to handle, place it in the bag, squeeze out some of the air, seal the bag, and marinate in the refrigerator, turning the beef occasionally, for at least 6 hours or up to 24 hours.

Place the bag in the freezer and freeze the beef for 20 minutes. Remove the beef from the bag and discard the marinade. Using a very sharp knife, cut the beef crosswise into even slices about ¼ inch (6 mm) thick. Arrange the slices on a platter or individual plates, scatter with the slivered green onions, and let stand for 10 minutes.

To make the citrus sauce, in a bowl, whisk together the soy sauce, vinegar, sugar, lemon juice, and chives. Spoon over the sliced beef and serve at once.

 **A NOTE FROM THE BUTCHER**

Beef tenderloin is the perfect cut to use in this recipe because you will be able to appreciate the tenderness of the meat. It is the most tender of all the beef cuts, but not the most flavorful, so it benefits from a full-bodied sauce like the one used here.

—Otto Demke, Gepperth's Meat Market, Chicago, IL

Although tri-tip is often grilled, I think that its leanness and stringy muscle structure make it a better candidate for stir-frying. When stir-fried, the meat can absorb the flavors of the other ingredients, rather than drying out from the heat of a grill. When you add the pieces of meat to the hot pan, be sure to distribute them evenly so that they brown nicely and cook uniformly. Cook the meat in batches, if necessary, to avoid overcrowding.

Place the beef on a baking sheet and freeze, uncovered, for 20 minutes. Meanwhile, core the radicchio. Cut lengthwise into quarters. Cut each quarter crosswise into thin slivers. Set aside.

Cut the beef in half lengthwise, then cut each half across the grain into slices about ¼ inch (6 mm) thick. Season the slices generously with salt and pepper.

Heat 1 tablespoon of the oil in a large wok or frying pan over medium-high heat until it is very hot. Add half the beef, distributing it evenly, and cook without moving it for about 20 seconds. Continue to cook the beef, tossing and stirring it every 15–20 seconds, until browned but still slightly pink inside, 2–3 minutes more. Transfer to a platter. Repeat to cook the remaining beef in the remaining 1 tablespoon oil, and transfer to the platter.

Pour off most of the oil from the pan. Reduce the heat to medium and add the butter. When the butter has foamed, add the radicchio and shallot, and toss and stir until the radicchio is wilted and tender, 3–4 minutes. Season with salt and pepper. Return the beef and any juices on the platter to the pan. Add the watercress and vinegar. Toss and stir for about 1 minute more to warm the beef. Serve at once.

# STIR-FRIED TRI-TIP WITH RADICCHIO

 MAKES 4 SERVINGS

1 tri-tip roast or top sirloin steak, about 1 lb (500 g)

1 large head radicchio, 8–9 oz (250–280 g)

Kosher salt and freshly ground pepper

2 tablespoons olive oil

2 tablespoons unsalted butter

1 large shallot, finely chopped

1 small bunch watercress or upland cress, tough stems removed

1 teaspoon white or red wine vinegar

---

## A NOTE FROM THE BUTCHER

The importance of cross-grain cutting when working with meat that has stringy muscle fibers— like tri-tip, flank steak, and skirt steak—cannot be stressed enough. Use your sharpest knife to cut perpendicularly through the fibers. This will ensure that the meat is tender, not chewy, when cooked.

—Robert Fleming, Alexander's Prime Meats and Catering, San Gabriel, CA

---

# STIR-FRIED FLANK STEAK WITH GREEN BEANS

 MAKES 4–6 SERVINGS

1 flank steak, 1¼–1½ lb (625–750 g)

¾ lb (375 g) green beans, trimmed

Kosher salt and freshly ground pepper

2 tablespoons canola oil

1 tablespoon peeled and grated fresh ginger

4 cloves garlic, minced

1 or 2 serrano chiles or 2 jalapeño chiles, seeded and very finely chopped

Juice of ½ lime

1 teaspoon Thai or Vietnamese fish sauce (optional)

Quick to prepare, healthful, and packed with flavor, this is the perfect dish to make for weeknight dinners. Although I love a well-marbled steak, I like flank steak for its leanness, its nice beefy flavor, and its toothsome bite. I often serve the stir-fry over steamed rice or quinoa, and pass lime wedges at the table for diners to squeeze over their portions. The jalapeño is milder than the serrano chile; adjust the quantity based on your affinity for fiery spice.

Place the beef on a baking sheet and freeze, uncovered, for 20 minutes. Meanwhile, bring a saucepan of lightly salted water to a boil. Add the beans and cook until barely tender, 4–5 minutes. Drain, rinse well under cold running water, and shake dry. Set aside.

Cut the beef in half lengthwise, then cut each half across the grain into slices about ¼ inch (6 mm) thick. Season the slices generously with salt and pepper.

Heat 1 tablespoon of the oil in a large frying pan or wok over medium-high heat until it is very hot. Add half the beef, distributing it evenly, and cook without moving it for about 20 seconds. Continue to cook the beef, tossing and stirring it every 15–20 seconds, until browned but still slightly pink inside, about 2 minutes more. Transfer to a platter. Repeat to cook the remaining beef in the remaining 1 tablespoon oil. Transfer to the platter.

Add the green beans, ginger, garlic, and chiles to the pan over medium-high heat, and toss and stir for 1 minute. Return the beef and any juices on the platter to the pan. Add the lime juice and fish sauce, if using. Season with salt and pepper. Toss and stir until heated through, 1–2 minutes. Serve at once.

---

### A NOTE FROM THE BUTCHER

Make sure to cut the flank steak across the grain, so that the stringlike muscle fibers are shortened, rendering the meat tender. Thinly sliced meat stir-fried over high heat can overcook quickly. Cooking it in small batches and allowing the pan to get very hot in between batches, ensures it will not overcook and the pieces will be nicely caramelized.

—Benjamin Dyer, Laurelhurst Market, Portland, OR

---

Grinding your own meat gives you control over the type of meat and quality of the cut used for burgers (see How to Grind Meat at Home, page 112). I think that hanger steak makes a far more delicious burger than run-of-the-mill chuck or round. Remember to use a light hand when forming the patties, and be careful not to compress the meat. The air pockets left in loosely packed patties hold all the delicious juices.

Arrange the steak cubes on a baking sheet and freeze, uncovered, for 20 minutes. Place one-third of the meat in a food processor and pulse about 12 times until coarsely chopped; don't let it turn to mush. You may have to redistribute the meat to achieve an even texture. Scrape out into a bowl without compacting the meat. Repeat to chop the remaining cubes.

Using a fork, mix the garlic powder and about ½ teaspoon pepper into the meat. With a light hand, form 4 loosely packed patties, then gently flatten them to about 1 inch (2.5 cm) thick and 3 inches (7.5 cm) in diameter. Refrigerate for 15 minutes.

Heat a 12-inch (30-cm) cast-iron frying pan over high heat until it is very hot, 2–3 minutes. Reduce the heat to medium-high, brush the tops of the burgers with oil, and season generously with salt. Place the burgers, oiled side down, in the pan and cook without moving them for 3 minutes. Brush the tops of the burgers with oil, season generously with salt, turn, and cook until an instant-read thermometer inserted into a burger registers 140°–145°F (60°–63°C) for medium, 5–7 minutes, or to your desired doneness (see page 20).

Place each burger and 1 or 2 toasted baguette slices on a plate. Top with a dollop of aioli and a dusting of fresh herbs. Serve at once.

# HOME-GROUND HANGER STEAK BURGERS

 MAKES 4 SERVINGS

1 hanger steak, about 1½ lb (750 g), trimmed of excess fat and cut into 1-inch (2.5-cm) cubes

½ teaspoon garlic powder

Kosher salt and freshly ground pepper

Olive oil for brushing

4–8 slices baguette, toasted until golden

Aioli (page 213)

1 tablespoon minced fresh herbs, such as tarragon, flat-leaf parsley, or basil

---

**A NOTE FROM THE BUTCHER**

Hanger steak is a small steak, usually only about 1 pound (500 g) or so, that hangs from the diaphragm of the steer. The cut has gained a following lately, so call your local butcher shop to make sure it is available. Don't purchase dry-aged steak for this recipe. Its flavor will be overpowering in the burgers.

—Paul Randolph, The Meat Shop, Phoenix, AZ

---

## MEXICAN-STYLE BEEF TARTARE

 MAKES 4 SERVINGS

1¼ lb (625 g) filet mignon, trimmed of excess fat and sinew

1 baguette, thinly sliced on the diagonal

Olive oil for brushing, plus 2 teaspoons

Kosher salt and freshly ground pepper

⅓ cup (2 oz/60 g) finely chopped red onion

⅓ cup (2½ oz/75 g) capers, rinsed and finely chopped

3 serrano chiles, seeded and very finely chopped

1½ tablespoons minced fresh cilantro

1 tablespoon Worcestershire sauce

1½ teaspoons Dijon mustard

Dash of hot-pepper sauce, such as Tabasco

4 small egg yolks

4 limes, quartered

Coarse sea salt for serving

The Mexican flavors used here—bright cilantro, hot serrano chiles, and refreshing lime juice—give new life to classic beef tartare. This salty, spicy, and fresh-tasting combination will win over any guest who may be reluctant to try raw beef.

Place the beef on a baking sheet and freeze, uncovered, for 20 minutes. Place a bowl and 4 plates in the freezer to chill.

Preheat the oven to 350°F (180°C). Brush the baguette slices lightly with olive oil and season with salt and pepper. Spread in a single layer on a baking sheet and toast until golden brown, about 10 minutes.

Cut the beef across the grain into thin slices. Stack the slices, a few at a time, and cut into thin strips. Stack a few strips and cut crosswise into a fine dice. In the very cold bowl, stir together the onion, capers, chiles, cilantro, Worcestershire sauce, mustard, 2 teaspoons oil, and a dash of hot-pepper sauce. Add the beef and mix with a fork to distribute the ingredients evenly; avoid compacting the beef.

Divide the mixture among the very cold plates. With the back of a spoon, make a well in the center of each serving. Gently deposit an egg yolk in each well. (Alternatively, leave each yolk in half of the shell and nestle in the meat; diners pour the yolk onto the meat and mix to incorporate.) Garnish with the lime quarters. Serve at once with the toasted baguette slices and with sea salt on the side for seasoning.

Note: If you choose to prepare beef raw, be sure to buy high-quality meat from a reputable butcher. Eating raw beef entails some degree of risk of bacterial contamination, including E. coli. The latter can make a healthy adult ill; the risk is greater for the very young, the elderly, pregnant women, or anyone with a compromised immune system. Eating raw eggs also carries some risk due to the threat of salmonella bacteria, though the incidence of contamination is extremely low. However, to be safe, the same people who should avoid raw beef should avoid raw eggs.

In Italy, this deceptively simple but highly flavorful dish is called *straccetti*, which means "little rags," a reference to the thinness of the pounded meat slices and the unevenness of the edges. You may need to order the extra-thick steak from your butcher, as this cut is not always readily available. The butcher can slice the meat for you, or you can seek out thin-sliced beef labeled for Japanese shabu-shabu, widely available at Asian markets.

## PANFRIED RIB EYE WITH ROASTED CHERRY PEPPERS

 MAKES 4–6 SERVINGS

To prepare the roasted cherry peppers, preheat the oven to 425°F (220°C). Place the peppers on a rimmed baking sheet and drizzle with the vinegar and olive oil. Scatter the garlic and oregano over the peppers and season with salt and pepper. Toss to coat evenly and spread in an even layer.

Roast for 30 minutes. Drizzle 2 tablespoons water over the peppers, toss, spread in an even layer, and continue to roast until the peppers are shriveled and slightly blackened but still juicy, about 20 minutes more. Set the baking sheet aside.

Place the steak on another baking sheet and freeze, uncovered, for 20 minutes. Cut the steak crosswise into slices about ⅓ inch (9 mm) thick. Place a piece of plastic wrap over each slice and pound it with a meat mallet or rolling pin until it is slightly less than ¼ inch (6 mm) thick. Season both sides of each slice generously with salt and pepper.

Warm the oil in a large frying pan over medium-high heat. Add the garlic and rosemary and sauté for about 1 minute. Add half of the beef and fry for 1 minute, without moving it around in the pan. Turn and fry for 30 seconds more. Transfer to a platter. Let the pan reheat for a few seconds, then repeat to fry the remaining beef. Transfer to the platter.

Top the beef with the rosemary and garlic from the pan and with the roasted peppers and their juices. Garnish with the parsley and serve at once.

### FOR THE ROASTED CHERRY PEPPERS

1 lb (500 g) sweet red and yellow cherry peppers

¼ cup (2 fl oz/60 ml) balsamic vinegar

3 tablespoons olive oil

1 large clove garlic, minced

¼ teaspoon dried oregano

Kosher salt and freshly ground pepper

1 boneless rib-eye steak, 1¾–2 lb (875 g–1 kg) and about 2 inches (5 cm) thick, trimmed of excess fat

Kosher salt and freshly ground pepper

2 tablespoons olive oil

6 large cloves garlic, smashed with the side of a heavy knife

4 fresh rosemary sprigs

1 tablespoon coarsely chopped fresh flat-leaf parsley

## NEW YORK STRIP STEAKS WITH HOMEMADE STEAK SAUCE

 MAKES 2 SERVINGS

For a splurge, purchase aged beef for this recipe. It has a rich and deeply complex flavor appreciated by many steak aficionados, myself included. Steak sauce is easy to make, keeps for months in the refrigerator, and tastes far better than bottled steak sauce. For a steak house–style meal, serve with Onion Rings (page 214) and sautéed spinach with a touch of cream and pinch of chile flakes.

**FOR THE STEAK SAUCE**

1 cup (8 oz/250 g) tomato ketchup

¼ cup (¼ oz/7 g) dried porcini mushrooms

¼ cup (2 fl oz/60 ml) Worcestershire sauce

¼ cup (2 fl oz/60 ml) fresh lemon juice

¼ cup (2 fl oz/60 ml) white vinegar

3 tablespoons Thai or Vietnamese fish sauce

½ cup (2½ oz/75 g) finely chopped white onion

1 clove garlic, minced

3 tablespoons reduced-sodium soy sauce

2 tablespoons firmly packed dark brown sugar

1 tablespoon dry mustard

2 boneless New York strip steaks, each about ¾ lb (375 g) and 1¼ inches (3 cm) thick

1 tablespoon olive oil, plus more for pan

Kosher salt

To make the steak sauce, in a saucepan, whisk together ¼ cup (2 fl oz/60 ml) water with the ketchup, mushrooms, Worcestershire sauce, lemon juice, vinegar, fish sauce, onion, garlic, soy sauce, sugar, and mustard. Bring to a boil, then reduce the heat, partially cover, and simmer gently until the sauce is thick, chunky, and very aromatic, about 45 minutes. Pass the sauce through a fine-mesh sieve to remove the solids. (The recipe makes 1½ cups/12 fl oz/375 ml. The sauce can be refrigerated for up to 2 months.)

Rub both sides of the steaks with the 1 tablespoon oil. Let stand at room temperature for 1 hour.

Heat a large, ovenproof frying pan over high heat until it is very hot, about 3 minutes. Season both sides of each steak generously with salt. Add enough oil to the pan to coat the bottom and reduce the heat to medium-high. When the oil is shimmering, use tongs to place the steaks in the pan without letting them touch. Sear without moving them for 2½ minutes. Turn the steaks and sear for 2 minutes more. Transfer to a rack set over a plate and let stand for at least 30 minutes or up to 1 hour.

About 30 minutes before serving, preheat the oven to 425°F (220°C). Return the steaks to the pan, place in the oven, and cook until an instant-read thermometer inserted into a steak registers 130°–135°F (54°–57°C) for medium-rare, 11–12 minutes, or to your desired doneness (see page 20). Transfer the steaks to the rack and let rest for about 5 minutes. Arrange the steaks on plates, top with some of the sauce, and serve at once.

---

**A NOTE FROM THE BUTCHER**

New York strips are best if cut from the rib-eye end rather than the sirloin side. The last three or four steaks near the sirloin side have a small cap muscle and corresponding piece of connective tissue separating the two muscles, which is why they are called two-toned. This results in a little tougher bite through that section.

—Mark Martin, Nelson's Meat Market, Cedar Rapids, IA

---

Also known as *bistecca alla Fiorentina*, this dish is named for the Tuscan city of Florence, is revered in Italy. The steak is slightly charred and smoky on the outside, gently perfumed with rosemary, and perfectly medium-rare on the inside. You know that the coals are ready when you can hold your hand just above the grill rack for only 4 seconds. For a welcome touch of acidity, I like to serve the steak with crunchy Endive Salad (page 215).

## GRILLED TUSCAN-STYLE STEAK

 | MAKES 2 OR 3 SERVINGS

1 well-marbled T-bone or porterhouse steak, 1¼–1½ inches (3–4 cm) thick, patted dry

Best-quality extra-virgin olive oil for brushing

3 fresh rosemary sprigs, tied together at the base to make a brush

Kosher salt and freshly ground pepper

Place the steak on a rimmed platter and drizzle generously with oil. Brush the oil into both sides with the rosemary brush. Let stand at room temperature for 1 hour, turning the steak and brushing it frequently with the rosemary.

Prepare a charcoal grill for direct-heat grilling over high heat, using hardwood charcoal. When the coals are covered with gray ash and the grill rack is very hot, season one side of the steak generously with salt. Place the steak on the rack, salted side down, over the hottest part of the fire and sear without moving it for 2 minutes. Season the top of the steak generously with salt, turn, and sear for 2 minutes more. Move the steak to a cooler part of the grill and continue to cook until an instant-read thermometer inserted into the steak, away from the bone, registers 130°–135°F (54°–57°C) for medium-rare, 9–12 minutes, or to your desired doneness (see page 20). Transfer the steak to a clean platter, brush with more olive oil, and season again with salt and pepper. Let rest, uncovered, for 5–7 minutes.

Cut the beef from the bone and then cut crosswise into thick slices. Drizzle with any juices from the platter and additional oil. Serve at once.

---

### A NOTE FROM THE BUTCHER

Porterhouse and T-bone steaks differ only in that they're cut from separate parts of the loin. They both include the New York strip and filet and are held together with a T-shaped bone that runs down the middle. The filet section of the porterhouse is larger than the filet on the T-bone.

—Jim Cascone, Huntington Meats, Los Angeles, CA

---

## PANFRIED BURGERS STUFFED WITH BLUE CHEESE

 MAKES 4 SERVINGS

Burgers with blue cheese in the center have been popular as long as the traditional hamburger has had a following. My only criticism of the stuffed burger is that it can't hold enough cheese to suit me, so I like to add more on top. Substitute any semisoft cheese such as Taleggio or Brie. Your butcher can grind the meat to order, but for superlative burgers, try grinding your own 20 percent beef chuck (see How to Grind Meat at Home, page 112).

1½ lb (750 g) ground beef chuck (20 percent fat), preferably ground at home or ground to order by the butcher

½ teaspoon garlic powder

Kosher salt and freshly ground pepper

¼ lb (125 g) very cold blue cheese, cut into 4 thin slabs, plus crumbled cheese for serving (optional)

Olive oil for brushing

Garlic Croûtes (page 213)

Sliced red onion and sliced tomato for serving (optional)

Aioli (page 213), mayonnaise, tomato ketchup, or mustard for serving (optional)

In a bowl, combine the ground chuck, the garlic powder, and ½ teaspoon pepper. Using a fork, stir together, keeping the mixture crumbly rather than compressed. With a light hand, form 8 loosely packed patties, then gently flatten each patty to about ½ inch (12 mm) thick and about 3 inches (7.5 cm) in diameter. Center a slab of blue cheese on each of 4 patties. Top with the remaining patties and press down with your palm until each double patty is about 1 inch (2.5 cm) thick. Press the edges together gently to seal in the cheese. Refrigerate for 15 minutes.

Heat a cast-iron frying pan over high heat until it is very hot, 2–3 minutes. Reduce the meat to medium-high, brush the tops of the burgers with oil, and season generously with salt. Place the burgers, oiled side down, and cook, without moving them, for 3 minutes. Brush the tops of the burgers with oil, season generously with salt, and turn and cook until an instant-read thermometer inserted into a burger registers 140°–145°F (60°–63°C) for medium, 5–7 minutes more, or to your desired doneness (see page 20). Arrange the burgers on plates with the croûtes, and set out the additional crumbled blue cheese, sliced onion and tomato, and the Aioli, mayonnaise, ketchup, and mustard (if using) for topping the burgers. Serve at once.

---

### A NOTE FROM THE BUTCHER

If grinding your own meat for this recipe, the crucial thing is to keep all your equipment very cold. Warm ground meat turns dense when cooked, whereas cold meat will give you fluffy and loose burgers. Keep all meat-grinding blades in the freezer until you are ready to grind, and let the ground meat pass directly into a very cold bowl.

—Joshua Applestone, Fleisher's Grass-fed & Organic Meats, Kingston, NY

---

Here, filet mignon, one of the most lauded cuts of beef, is cooked first on the stove top, then finished in the oven. The Parmesan butter melts over the warm meat, complementing its richness and adding an appealing nuttiness. Don't use a nonstick pan for this recipe. It cannot safely achieve the heat level necessary for excellent browning. When making this recipe at the height of summer, accompany it with Tomato-Basil Salad (page 215).

## FILETS MIGNONS WITH PARMESAN BUTTER

 MAKES 4 SERVINGS

To make the Parmesan butter, in a mini food processor, combine the butter, the cheese, ¼ teaspoon salt, and ¼ teaspoon cracked pepper. Pulse until smooth. Set aside at room temperature. (The butter can be tightly covered and refrigerated for up to 2 weeks; return to room temperature before serving.)

Rub both sides of the steaks with oil. Let stand for 1 hour at room temperature.

Heat a large, ovenproof frying pan over high heat until it is very hot, about 3 minutes. Season both sides of each steak generously with salt and pepper. Add enough oil to the pan to coat the bottom and reduce the heat to medium-high. When the oil is shimmering, use tongs to place the steaks in the pan without letting them touch. Cook without moving them for 2½ minutes. Turn the steaks and cook for 2 minutes more. Transfer to a rack set over a plate and let stand for at least 30 minutes or up to 1 hour.

Preheat the oven to 425°F (220°C). Return the steaks to the pan, place in the oven, and cook until an instant-read thermometer inserted into a steak registers 130°–135°F (54°–57°C) for medium-rare, 11–12 minutes, or to your desired doneness (see page 20). Transfer the steaks to the rack and let rest, uncovered, for 3–5 minutes.

Arrange the steaks on plates, top each with a large spoonful of Parmesan butter, and serve at once.

### FOR THE PARMESAN BUTTER

6 tablespoons (3 oz/90 g) unsalted butter, at room temperature, cut into chunks

½ cup (2 oz/60 g) grated Parmigiano-Reggiano cheese

Kosher salt and coarsely cracked pepper

4 filets mignons, each about ¾ lb (375 g) and 1½ inches (4 cm) thick, patted dry

Olive oil for coating and for pan

Kosher salt and freshly ground pepper

# BEEF SATAY WITH PEANUT-COCONUT SAUCE

 MAKES 6 SERVINGS

Grilling meat on skewers is such an ingenious way to cook and serve bite-sized morsels that many cultures around the world have their own variations. *Satay*, a Southeast Asian specialty, is similar to brochettes in France, *spiedini* in Italy, kebabs in the Middle East, and souvlaki in Greece. The tart-sweet sauce with a hint of spice and a squeeze of lime provide a superb complement to the crisp-crusted meat.

1¾ lb (875 g) beef chuck, trimmed of excess fat and cut into 1-inch (2.5 cm) cubes

1½ teaspoons curry powder

1 tablespoon peanut or canola oil

Kosher salt and freshly ground pepper

### FOR THE PEANUT-COCONUT SAUCE

2 tablespoons peanut or canola oil

2 tablespoons minced white or yellow onion

4 cloves garlic, minced

½ teaspoon hot-pepper sauce, such as Tabasco

1 tablespoon firmly packed dark brown sugar

1 tablespoon fresh lime juice

½ cup (2½ oz/75 g) roasted peanuts, finely chopped

Kosher salt and freshly ground pepper

1 cup (8 fl oz/250 ml) unsweetened coconut milk

1 tablespoon minced fresh cilantro

Lime wedges for finishing

In a large bowl, combine the beef cubes with the curry powder, the oil, ½ teaspoon salt, and plenty of pepper. Toss to coat the beef evenly. Let stand at room temperature while you make the sauce. If using bamboo skewers, soak 12 skewers in water to cover.

To make the peanut-coconut sauce, in a frying pan over medium heat, warm the oil. Add the onion and cook, stirring, until softened but not browned, about 5 minutes. Add the garlic and cook for 1 minute more. Stir in the hot-pepper sauce, brown sugar, lime juice, and peanuts. Season with ¼ teaspoon salt and a pinch of pepper. Stir in the coconut milk and continue to cook, stirring frequently, until thickened, 6–8 minutes. Remove from the heat and stir in the cilantro.

Prepare a charcoal or gas grill for direct-heat grilling over medium-high heat, or preheat a stove-top cast-iron grill pan over medium-high heat. Thread the beef cubes onto the skewers, dividing them evenly and pressing them together snugly. Wrap 2 inches (5 cm) of the blunt end of each skewer with aluminum foil to make a handle. Place the skewers on the grill rack over the hottest part of the fire, or in the grill pan, and cook, turning them with tongs, until the meat is firm but still has a little give, 3½–4 minutes per side. Transfer to a platter and let rest, loosely covered, for 3–4 minutes.

Remove the foil from the skewers. Squeeze a little lime juice over the top. Serve at once with the sauce on the side.

---

**A NOTE FROM THE BUTCHER**

When the cooking method is quick, hot, and dry, it's best to use a cut with generous marbling, like the chuck in this recipe, so that the meat stays moist and flavorful. You could also choose round or tri-tip if you prefer leaner meat, but those cuts can toughen on the grill.

—Ryan Farr, 4505 Meats, San Francisco, CA

---

Boneless rib eye tends to be tough when cooked rare, so I suggest grilling these steaks to medium-rare. Here, I use a lemon-scented olive oil as the final flavoring for these earthy-flavored steaks, which pair beautifully with the refreshing Fennel-Parsley Slaw on page 215. To make lemon olive oil, combine ½ cup (4 fl oz/125 ml) extra-virgin olive oil with the finely grated zest of 1 lemon. Let stand for at least 30 minutes before using.

Remove the steaks from the refrigerator and let stand at room temperature for 1 hour.

Prepare a charcoal or gas grill for direct-heat grilling over high heat, or preheat a cast-iron stove-top grill pan over high heat. Brush both sides of each steak with oil and rub with the paprika. Season one side of each steak generously with salt. Place the steaks, salted side down, on the grill rack over the hottest part of the fire or in the grill pan, and cook without moving them for 2 minutes. Move the steaks after 1 minute if the fire flares. Turn, season the cooked sides with salt, and cook for 2 minutes more. Move the steaks to a cooler part of the grill or reduce the heat, and continue to cook until an instant-read thermometer inserted into a steak registers 130°–135°F (54° 57°C) for medium-rare, about 8 minutes more, or to your desired doneness (see page 20). Turn the steaks several times to brown the crust on both sides. Transfer to a platter and season both sides generously with pepper. Tent loosely with aluminum foil and let rest for 4–5 minutes.

Drizzle the steaks with lemon oil and squeeze lemon juice over the top. Serve at once.

# GRILLED RIB-EYE STEAKS WITH PAPRIKA RUB

 **MAKES 4 SERVINGS**

3 or 4 well-marbled boneless rib-eye steaks, each about 1½ inches (4 cm) thick

Lemon olive oil for brushing and drizzling

1½ teaspoons smoked paprika

Kosher salt and freshly ground pepper

Lemon wedges for finishing

**A NOTE FROM THE BUTCHER**

The amount of marbling in a rib-eye steak is what sets it apart from other steaks and gives it a signature flavor. The marbling can vary, depending on whether the steak is cut from the shoulder end or the loin end. When cut from the loin end, the steaks resemble New York strip steaks, as the loin is the source of strip steaks. Ask your butcher for steaks cut from the shoulder end to get that true rib eye flavor.

—Bryan Flannery, Bryan's Fine Foods, San Francisco, CA

## PAN-ROASTED PORTERHOUSE STEAK

 MAKES 2 OR 3 SERVINGS

The slightly unconventional cooking method here would be familiar to a steak-house chef. The sequence of initial high-heat sear, long rest, and oven finish allows the tasty juices to remain in the meat while the heat migrates slowly toward the center in what is known as residual-heat cooking (see page 12). I'm convinced that once you try this method, it will become part of your cooking repertoire. Serve with Creamy White Beans (page 214).

1 porterhouse steak, about 1½ lb (750 g) and 1¼–1½ inches (3–4 cm) thick, patted dry

1 tablespoon olive oil, plus more for serving

Kosher salt and freshly ground pepper

Rub both sides of the steak with the 1 tablespoon oil. Let stand at room temperature for 1–1½ hours.

Heat a large, ovenproof frying pan over high heat until it is very hot, about 3 minutes. Season one side of the steak generously with salt. Add enough oil to the pan to coat the bottom and reduce the heat to medium-high. When the oil is shimmering, use tongs to place the steak in the pan, salted side down, and let cook without moving it for 2½ minutes. Season the top with salt, turn, and season with pepper to your liking. Cook for 2½ minutes more. Transfer to a rack set over a plate and let stand at room temperature for at least 30 minutes or up to 1 hour.

Preheat the oven to 425°F (220°C). Return the steak to the pan, place in the oven, and cook until an instant-read thermometer inserted into the steak away from the bone registers 130°–135°F (54°–57°C) for medium-rare, about 12 minutes, or to your desired doneness (see page 20). Transfer to the rack and let rest, uncovered, for 5–8 minutes.

Cut the sirloin away from the bone on one side and the filet section on the other. Cut across the grain into thick slices. Arrange on plates. Serve at once, passing oil at the table for drizzling.

### A NOTE FROM THE BUTCHER

When you are cooking a bone-in steak such as a porterhouse, keep in mind that the area around the bone will cook more slowly than the rest of the meat. Always remember to check the internal temperature close to the center of the steak (but away from the bone) to get an accurate reading. This way, you can make sure that your steak is cooked to perfection.

—Erika Nakamura, Lindy and Grundy's Meats, Los Angeles, CA

Many chefs—even committed enthusiasts of rare steak—believe that rib-eye steaks are more delicious when cooked to medium-rare rather than very rare or rare. Rib eye has more marbling than New York strip, T-bone, and porterhouse steaks, and since fat carries flavor, the rib eye is, in my opinion, the tastiest steak of all.

To make the chipotle-lime butter, place the butter, chile and sauce, and lime zest and juice in a food processor. Add ¼ teaspoon salt and a grinding or two of pepper. Process, scraping down the bowl as necessary, until blended thoroughly. Add the cilantro and pulse to blend. Place a 30-inch (76-cm) piece of plastic wrap on a work surface. Place large dollops of the butter down the center, spacing them close together. Bring up a long side of the plastic wrap and use it to gently mold and smooth the butter into a cylinder about 1 inch (2.5 cm) in diameter. Wrap securely in the plastic and freeze for at least 30 minutes or up to 1 month. If the butter has been frozen for longer than 1 hour, remove it from the freezer 30 minutes before serving.

Remove the steaks from the refrigerator and let stand at room temperature for 1 hour.

Prepare a charcoal or gas grill for direct-heat grilling over high heat, or preheat a cast-iron stove-top grill pan over high heat. Brush both sides of each steak sparingly with oil. Season one side generously with salt. Place the steaks, salted side down, on the grill rack over the hottest part of the fire, or in the grill pan, and cook without moving them for 2½ minutes. Move the steaks after 1 minute if the fire flares up. Season the tops of the steaks with salt, turn, and cook for 2½ minutes more. Move the steaks to a cooler part of the grill or reduce the heat to medium, and continue to cook until an instant-read thermometer inserted into a steak away from the bone registers 130°–135°F (54°–57°C) for medium-rare, about 9 minutes, or to your desired doneness (see page 20). Turn the steaks several times to brown the crust on both sides. Transfer the steaks to a platter and season both sides generously with pepper. Tent loosely with aluminum foil and let rest for 3–4 minutes.

Arrange the steaks on plates, top each steak with a slice of the chipotle butter, and garnish with a lime wedge. Serve at once.

## GRILLED RIB-EYE STEAKS WITH CHIPOTLE-LIME BUTTER

 MAKES 4 SERVINGS

**FOR THE CHIPOTLE-LIME BUTTER**

1 cup (8 oz/250 g) unsalted butter, at room temperature, cut into chunks

1 canned chipotle chile in adobo, plus 1 teaspoon adobo sauce

Zest of 1 lime, removed in strips with a vegetable peeler

2 teaspoons fresh lime juice

Kosher salt and freshly ground pepper

2 tablespoons minced fresh cilantro

4 well-marbled bone-in rib-eye steaks, each about 1 lb (500 g) and 1½ inches (4 cm) thick

Olive oil for brushing

Lime wedges for serving

# HOW TO MAKE JERKY

### BEST CUTS FOR JERKY

Since fat will turn rancid, extremely lean cuts of meat are the best choices for jerky. The round section of any animal, from the top of the leg, is often passed up for roasting or even braising because of its extreme leanness, but this same attribute makes it an excellent candidate for jerky. Any cut from the round section will work well. Top round is slightly more tender than eye of round and bottom round, but after the meat is cured, the difference is barely noticeable.

### ALTERNATIVE DRYING METHODS

If you have a smoker, you can use it to dry the marinated meat. When preparing the marinade, omit the Liquid Smoke. After the meat is placed in the smoker, maintain the temperature at 170°–190°F (77°–88°C). You can also dry the meat in a dehydrator: set at 145°F (63°C). For both of these drying methods, be sure that the meat slices do not overlap on the rack. Dry the meat for 4–6 hours.

### OTHER MEATS TO JERKY

Lean cuts of lamb, from the leg or the loin, can make fine jerky and taste especially good when marinated with spicy or fruity ingredients. Hunters often make jerky from venison, elk, and other lean game meats. Of the many recipes available, favorite flavors range from teriyaki to incendiary chile.

Long before refrigeration methods were invented, people looked for ways to preserve meat, especially from an animal too large to consume at one meal. They discovered that salt both inhibits spoilage and draws moisture from meat. Preserving with salt made the meat nonperishable and lighter in weight, ideal for transporting on long journeys. For today's home cook, jerky is probably the easiest preserved meat to prepare. Homemade jerky is also vastly superior in texture and flavor to the store-bought product.

**SLICING THE MEAT**  Place the meat on a baking sheet and freeze it for 45 minutes. The meat will become firm, making it easier to slice. With a long, flexible, very sharp knife, cut the meat into slices ⅛–¼ inch (3–6 mm) thick (comparable to thick-cut bacon). If you cut the meat paper-thin, it will be too brittle. For traditional jerky, cut the meat with the grain. For jerky that is easier to chew, cut it across the grain.

**MARINATING THE MEAT**  After combining the marinade ingredients in a large, sturdy resealable plastic bag, add the meat slices in batches, massaging after each addition to coat both sides of each slice and distribute the marinade evenly. Squeeze out most of the air from the bag and seal. Refrigerate for 6 hours but no more than 8 hours. Turn the bag and massage it every 2 hours, moving the slices around. Drain the slices in a colander and discard the marinade. Blot both sides of each slice thoroughly dry with paper towels.

**DRYING THE MEAT**  Line the floor of the oven with heavy-duty aluminum foil, covering it completely and folding up the edges of the foil to form a rim that will help contain the drippings. Spray the oven racks lightly with nonstick cooking spray. Arrange the slices directly on the racks, spacing them about ¼ inch (6 mm) apart. Set the oven temperature to 170°F (77°C). Use a folded kitchen towel to prop the oven door open by just under 1 inch (2.5 cm), to allow the moisture to escape. Let the meat dry for 2 hours. Turn the slices and continue to dry them for 1–2 hours more. The timing will depend on the moisture content of the meat, the ambient humidity, and the temperature of the oven. When the meat is done, it should be firm and dry, but still flexible.

**STORING THE JERKY**  Store-bought jerky will keep at room temperature because it contains preservatives and has been dried very thoroughly for optimum safety. Homemade jerky is moister and is best stored in a resealable bag in the refrigerator. Inspect the meat frequently. Because the center of the jerky dries more slowly than the exterior, you may see wet spots within the first few days after the meat was dried. If you do, open the bag and leave it in direct sunlight for 1 hour or so to finish drying. If any green mold develops, or the meat smells spoiled, discard it.

## CLASSIC BEEF JERKY

MAKES ABOUT 1 LB (500 G)

3 lb (1.5 kg) eye of round, top round, or bottom round beef, trimmed of all exterior fat

⅔ cup (5 fl oz/160 ml) soy sauce, preferably tamari or fermented

⅓ cup (3 fl oz/80 ml) Angostura or orange bitters

2 teaspoons Liquid Smoke (optional)

1–2 teaspoons hot-pepper sauce

1 teaspoon freshly ground pepper

1 teaspoon garlic powder

1 teaspoon onion powder

Cut the meat into slices as directed at left. In a large, sturdy, resealable plastic bag, combine the soy sauce, bitters, Liquid Smoke (if using), hot-pepper sauce, pepper, and garlic and onion powders. Follow the directions at left for marinating, drying, and storing the meat. The jerky should be consumed within 6 weeks.

### SWEET THAI JERKY MARINADE

In a large, sturdy resealable plastic bag, combine ¼ cup (3 oz/90 g) honey, 5 tablespoons (3 fl oz/80 ml) soy sauce, 3 tablespoons fish sauce, 2 tablespoons ground coriander, and 1 tablespoon ground lemongrass.

### RUM-GINGER JERKY MARINADE

In a small saucepan, simmer ⅔ cup (5 fl oz/160 ml) dark rum for 5 minutes to burn off the alcohol. Transfer to a bowl and stir in ½ cup (4 fl oz/125 ml) fresh lime juice, ¼ cup (2 fl oz/60 ml) soy sauce, 2 tablespoons Worcestershire sauce, 2 teaspoons Liquid Smoke (optional), 1 teaspoon hot-pepper sauce, and a 2-inch (5-cm) piece of fresh ginger, peeled and grated. Transfer to a large, sturdy resealable plastic bag. To help soak up any remaining alcohol, sprinkle the meat slices with coarse salt before drying.

## GRILLED SKIRT STEAK WITH CHIMICHURRI

 MAKES 6 OR 7 SERVINGS

Lean, but possessed of a deep beef flavor and pleasantly chewy texture, skirt steak is long and narrow and will require a little dexterity to manage on the grill. Like flank steak, it should be sliced across the grain for maximum juiciness. Piquant *chimichurri* is emerald green from the abundance of parsley and tart from the vinegar. The sauce is ubiquitous on tables in Argentina, where beef and other meats are a centerpiece of the cuisine.

1 skirt steak, about 3 lb (1.5 kg)

2 tablespoons olive oil

Kosher salt and freshly ground pepper

### FOR THE CHIMICHURRI

1½ cups (about 2 oz/60 g) firmly packed fresh flat-leaf parsley leaves and tender stems

6 cloves garlic

3 tablespoons fresh oregano leaves

¾ cup (6 fl oz/180 ml) olive oil

Kosher salt and freshly ground black pepper

⅛–¼ teaspoon red pepper flakes

3 tablespoons red wine vinegar

Place the steak in a large nonreactive baking dish. Brush both sides with the oil and season generously with salt and pepper. Cover with plastic wrap and refrigerate for at least 1 hour or up to 6 hours.

To prepare the *chimichurri*, in a food processor, combine the parsley, garlic, and oregano. Process to chop finely. Alternatively, chop by hand. Transfer to a bowl and stir in the olive oil, 2 teaspoons salt, 1 teaspoon black pepper, and the pepper flakes. Cover and refrigerate for at least 1 hour or up to 6 hours.

Remove the steak and the *chimichurri* from the refrigerator and let stand at room temperature for about 45 minutes. Prepare a charcoal or gas grill for direct-heat grilling over high heat, or preheat a cast-iron stove-top grill pan over high heat. Place the steak on the grill rack over the hottest part of the fire or in the grill pan, and cook without moving it for about 1½ minutes. Turn and cook until an instant-read thermometer inserted into the steak registers 130°–135°F (54°–57°C) for medium-rare, 1–3 minutes more, or to your desired doneness (see page 20). Transfer the steak to a platter and let rest, loosely covered, for about 5 minutes.

Stir the vinegar into the *chimichurri*. Cut the steak across the grain and on the diagonal into slices about ½ inch (12 mm) thick. Top with the some of the *chimichurri* and serve at once, passing the remaining *chimichurri* at the table.

### A NOTE FROM THE BUTCHER

For an alternative to skirt steak, ask for hanger, flap, or flank steak. My favorite cut for everyday grilling is flap meat, also called bavette steak. It is well marbled, tasty, and affordable. To ensure that the meat remains moist while grilling, ask your butcher to leave the meat "unpeeled."

—Tia Harrison, Avedano's Holly Park Market, San Francisco, CA

Sirloin is less marbled than more luxurious cuts like strip loin and New York strip, but has great flavor and is the perfect cut to slice and use in a simple salad. Gorgonzola adds a rich tang, and the peppery arugula complements the seasoned meat. To toast the pine nuts, warm them in a small, dry frying pan over medium heat. Toast the nuts for a minute or two, jiggling the pan to avoid scorching, until the nuts start to brown lightly.

# SIRLOIN STEAK SALAD WITH GORGONZOLA AND PINE NUTS

 MAKES 4 SERVINGS

Rub both sides of the steaks with 1 tablespoon of the oil. Season both sides generously with salt and pepper. Rub some of the rosemary into both sides of each steak. Let stand at room temperature for 1 hour. Or, preferably, refrigerate uncovered for 4 hours and remove from the refrigerator about 40 minutes before cooking.

Prepare a charcoal or gas grill for direct-heat grilling over medium-high heat, or preheat a cast-iron stove-top grill pan over high heat. Place the steaks on the grill rack over the hottest part of the fire or in the grill pan, and cook without moving them for 2½ minutes. Move them after 1 minute if the fire flares up. Turn and cook for 2½ minutes. Move the steaks to a cooler part of the grill or reduce the heat to medium, and continue to cook until a thermometer inserted into a steak registers 120°–125°F (49°–52°C) for rare, about 5 minutes, or to your desired doneness (see page 20). Transfer to a platter and let stand, loosely covered, for at least 10 minutes or up to 30 minutes.

Meanwhile, in a bowl, whisk together the vinegar, mustard, garlic, ½ teaspoon salt, and plenty of pepper. Whisking constantly, add the remaining 4 tablespoons oil in a thin stream and continue to whisk until emulsified.

Arrange the greens in a large serving bowl. Cut the steaks across the grain into slices about ½ inch (12 mm) thick. Arrange on the salad. Top with the pine nuts and Gorgonzola, drizzle with the dressing, and serve at once.

2 sirloin steaks, each about 1 lb (500 g) and 1 inch (2.5 cm) thick

5 tablespoons (3 fl oz/80 ml) olive oil

Kosher salt and freshly ground pepper

2 teaspoons minced fresh rosemary

1 tablespoon red wine vinegar

2 teaspoons Dijon mustard

1 large clove garlic, minced

8 cups (½ lb/250 g) mixed baby greens

3 tablespoons pine nuts, toasted

6 oz (185 g) Gorgonzola cheese, crumbled

## A NOTE FROM THE BUTCHER

If you're feeding a crowd and want to save a little money, you can use top round in place of the sirloin. Ask your butcher for inside top round, a nice cut from the round that is often less expensive than sirloin. You won't have to alter the cooking method.

—James Cross, Marczyk Fine Foods, Denver, CO

## ROASTED BEEF, ARUGULA, AND TANGERINE SALAD

 MAKES 8–10 SERVINGS

For a long time, I avoided using cuts from the round section, as I felt it lacked enough marbling to make the cooked meat tasty and tender. But after experimenting with different cuts, I discovered that the round is ideal for roast beef, especially when the meat is thinly sliced and served cold. The low-and-slow approach used here yields slices that are evenly pink, moist, and supple, perfect for sandwiches or this bracing, tart-sweet salad.

1 top round roast, about 4 lb (2 kg), fat trimmed to ¼ inch (6 mm), patted dry

Olive oil for brushing

Kosher salt and freshly ground pepper

2 oz (60 g) fatback or salt pork, thinly sliced (optional)

1 large red onion, thinly sliced lengthwise, then cut crosswise into ½-inch (12-mm) pieces

Ice water

### FOR THE VINAIGRETTE

¼ cup (2 fl oz/60 ml) white wine vinegar

2 tablespoons Dijon mustard

2 teaspoons coarsely cracked peppercorns

Kosher salt

¾ cup (6 fl oz/180 ml) extra-virgin olive oil

5 tangerines, peel and pith removed with a sharp knife, cut into segments between the membranes, and diced

1 lb (500 g) baby arugula

Remove the roast from the refrigerator and let stand at room temperature for 2 hours.

Preheat the oven to 450°F (230°C). Brush the roast lightly with oil and season generously all over with salt and pepper. Place the roast, fat side up, on a rack in a roasting pan. If using the fatback, lay the slices over the top. Place in the oven and cook for 20 minutes. Reduce the oven temperature to 300°F (150°C) and continue to cook until an instant-read thermometer inserted into the center of the roast registers 130°–135°F (54°–57°C) for medium-rare, 1¾–2 hours more. Remove the roast from the oven and let stand, loosely covered, for at least 25 minutes. Meanwhile, put the onion in a bowl, add ice water to cover, and let stand for 30–45 minutes to crisp the onion and mellow the flavor.

To make the vinaigrette, in a large bowl, whisk together the vinegar, mustard, peppercorns, and 1 teaspoon salt. Whisking constantly, drizzle in the olive oil, and continue to whisk until the mixture is emulsified.

Drain the onion well and pat dry. Add the onion, tangerines, and arugula to the vinaigrette and toss gently.

Discard the fatback and the string from the roast, if any. Cut the roast into large, even slices about ¼ inch (6 mm) thick. Divide the salad among bowls and arrange the beef slices on top. Serve at once.

---

### A NOTE FROM THE BUTCHER

The day before you roast the beef for this salad, pat it dry with paper towels, rub it liberally with salt, place on a rack in a roasting pan, and let rest, uncovered, in the refrigerator overnight. This process wicks away moisture from the outside of the roast, allowing the meat to absorb more flavors during roasting. The salt also penetrates the meat, giving it a well-seasoned flavor throughout.

—Benjamin Dyer, Laurelhurst Market, Portland, OR

---

I never thought any preparation for flank steak could top my mother's, which called for soaking the steak in a soy-mustard marinade before cooking. But this hybrid of the classic Argentinean *matambre* with the Italian *braciole* has won me over. All my favorite flavors are in this dish: the tasty meat, prosciutto (for that heavenly cured-pork accent), bright green herbs, salty sheep's milk cheese, and briny green olives.

To butterfly the flank steak, place the steak at the edge of a cutting board with a short side toward you and the edge of the narrower long side on your right (reverse if you are left-handed). Using a long, thin-bladed knife, cut the meat almost in half through the narrower side, from right to left (or vice versa). Open it as you would a book. With a mallet, pound the steak lightly to an even thickness. Ideally, you want a rough square of meat that is 12–15 inches (30–38 cm).

Preheat the oven to 350°F (180°C).

Lightly season the cut side of the meat with salt and pepper. Lay the prosciutto slices in an even layer running across the grain from top to bottom. In a bowl, combine the garlic, oregano, sage, olives, cheese, bread crumbs, vinegar, and 2 tablespoons of the oil. Stir to blend evenly. Spread the mixture evenly over the prosciutto, leaving 3 inches (7.5 cm) of one side of the meat uncovered. Roll up the meat around the filling, working toward the uncovered side, to make a compact roll. The roll should be about 4 inches (10 cm) in diameter. Tie it at regular intervals with kitchen string.

Choose a roasting pan large enough to accommodate the rolled meat. Place the pan on the stove top over medium-high heat, and warm the remaining 1 tablespoon oil. Add the roll and cook, turning as needed, until browned well on all sides, 12–15 minutes total. Place in the oven and cook until an instant-read thermometer inserted into the center of the roll registers 130°–135°F (54°–57°C) for medium-rare, 25–30 minutes. Transfer to a cutting board, tent loosely with aluminum foil, and let rest for 15–30 minutes.

Snip the strings and cut into slices ¾–1 inch (2–2.5 cm) thick. Serve at once.

# ROASTED FLANK STEAK STUFFED WITH OLIVES AND PECORINO

 MAKES 6–8 SERVINGS

1 flank steak, 1½–1¾ lb (750–875 g)

Kosher salt and freshly ground pepper

5 very thin slices prosciutto

6 cloves garlic, minced

3 tablespoons coarsely chopped fresh oregano

1 tablespoon minced fresh sage

1 can (about 5 oz/165 g) anchovy-stuffed green olives, drained and finely chopped, or 1¼ cups (6 oz/185 g) brine-cured green olives, pitted and coarsely chopped

6 oz (185 g) *pecorino romano* cheese, grated

¾ cup (1½ oz/45 g) seasoned dried bread crumbs, toasted until golden, or Toasted Garlic Bread Crumbs (page 213)

1 tablespoon red wine vinegar

3 tablespoons extra-virgin olive oil

**A NOTE FROM THE BUTCHER**

Any recipe calling for flank steak can be executed with skirt, hanger, flat iron, or top cap steak. These cuts cook similarly, but each has a unique grain. Try them side by side with the same cooking technique to discover the differences on your own.

—Wayne Schroeder, Clancey's Meats and Fish, Minneapolis, MN

## FLANK STEAK SANDWICHES WITH TOMATO CHUTNEY

 MAKES 6 SERVINGS

The full-bodied combination of ingredients in this sandwich—Manchego cheese, arugula, and a piquant chutney seasoned with sherry vinegar—owes much to the Spanish countryside. The beefiness of flank steak stands up well to refrigeration, so grilling the night before is a great option for serving the sandwiches at a picnic.

### FOR THE TOMATO CHUTNEY

1 large shallot, finely chopped

1 large canned chipotle chile in adobo, plus 1–2 teaspoons adobo sauce

3 tablespoons sherry vinegar

2 tablespoons firmly packed dark brown sugar

Kosher salt

6 canned San Marzano tomatoes, drained, seeded, and cut into ¾-inch (2-cm) chunks

¼ teaspoon Worcestershire sauce

1 flank steak, about 1 lb (500 g)

1½ tablespoons olive oil

Kosher salt and freshly ground pepper

6 pieces plain focaccia, each about 3 inches (7.5 cm) square, split horizontally

6 oz (185 g) Manchego or aged pecorino cheese, thinly sliced

2 cups (2 oz/60 g) baby arugula

⅓ cup (3 fl oz/80 ml) mayonnaise

To prepare the chutney, in a saucepan over medium-low heat, combine the shallot, chile and sauce, vinegar, brown sugar, and ¼ teaspoon salt. Bring to a simmer, stirring. Cover and cook until the shallot is softened, about 5 minutes. Stir in the tomatoes and Worcestershire sauce. Partially cover the pan and cook, stirring frequently, until the mixture thickens, 10–15 minutes. Let cool.

Place the flank steak in a large baking dish and brush both sides with the oil. Season generously with salt and pepper. Let stand for at least 1 hour at room temperature or up to 3 hours in the refrigerator. If the steak is refrigerated, bring to room temperature before grilling.

Prepare a charcoal or gas grill for direct-heat grilling over medium-high heat, or preheat a cast-iron stove-top grill pan over high heat. Place the steak on the grill rack over the hottest part of the fire, or in the grill pan, and cook without moving it for 5 minutes. Turn and cook until an instant-read thermometer inserted into the steak registers 130°–135°F (54°–57°C) for medium-rare, 4–6 minutes, or to your desired doneness (see page 20). Transfer to a cutting board and let rest for 5 minutes.

Cut the steak against the grain into thin slices. Spread the chutney on the focaccia bottoms. Layer with the sliced flank steak, cheese, and arugula. Spread the focaccia tops lightly with the mayonnaise and place on the sandwiches. Serve at once.

### A NOTE FROM THE BUTCHER

Flank steak is the fibrous muscle located on the inside wall of the beef flank. The meat is tender and juicy. It is ideal for recipes that call for the meat to be cut on the bias or sliced after cooking. Select a flank steak that is short and thick with some of the white fat still remaining. The longer flank steaks are usually chewy.

—Frank Castrogiovanni, Ottomanelli Brothers, New York, NY

Rib roast is a decadent cut with generous marbling. The rich veins of fat melt during roasting and baste the meat from the inside out, creating juicy results. I call anchovies "rustic salt." Here, they team up with garlic to permeate the meat with an earthy flavor that cuts through the richness. Mustard and bread crumbs add a satisfying crunch to the golden exterior.

Remove the roast from the refrigerator and let stand at room temperature for 1½ hours.

Preheat the oven to 500°F (260°C). Cut slits about ½ inch (12 mm) deep all over the roast, spacing them about 2 inches (5 cm) apart. Cut each anchovy crosswise into small pieces. Insert a sliver of garlic and a piece of anchovy into each slit. Place the roast, fat side up, on a rack in a roasting pan. Brush the top lightly with oil and season all sides generously with salt. Place in the oven and cook until the fat is sizzling and golden, about 20 minutes.

Meanwhile, prepare the crust: In a bowl, whisk together the oil, mustard, thyme, bread crumbs, and plenty of pepper.

Remove the roast from the oven and, using the back of a spoon, press the crust mixture over the top of the beef, compressing it into a firm layer. Reduce the oven temperature to 325°F (165°C). Return the roast to the oven and continue to cook until an instant-read thermometer inserted into the roast registers 130°–135°F (54°–57°C) for medium-rare, 1¼–1½ hours, or to your desired doneness (see page 20). Transfer the roast to a platter, tent loosely with aluminum foil, and let rest for 8–10 minutes. Carve into thin slices. Serve at once, accompanied by the lemon wedges.

# RIB-EYE ROAST WITH MUSTARD AND BREAD CRUMB CRUST

 MAKES 6–8 SERVINGS

1 boneless rib-eye roast, 3½–4 lb (1.75–2 kg), fat trimmed to about ¼ inch (6 mm)

6 anchovy fillets, soaked in water for 10 minutes, drained, and patted dry

4 cloves garlic, cut into thin slivers

Olive oil for brushing

Kosher salt

**FOR THE CRUST**

3 tablespoons olive oil

⅓ cup (3 oz/90 g) whole-grain mustard

1 tablespoon dried thyme

1 cup (2 oz/60 g) fresh bread crumbs

Freshly ground pepper

Lemon wedges for serving

---

**A NOTE FROM THE BUTCHER**

For anyone who has ever struggled when carving a traditional rib roast, this is a neat trick: Ask your butcher to remove the ribs, but tie them back on. The cooking process will be exactly the same, without any loss of juice. When the roast is done, you simply cut the strings and lift the meat away—you'll have a boneless roast to slice, and you can cut up the ribs and serve them alongside the sliced meat.

—Bryan Flannery, Bryan's Fine Foods, San Francisco, CA

---

## KOREAN-STYLE SHORT RIBS

 MAKES 6 SERVINGS

The classic flavors of soy sauce and fish sauce provide a satisfying balance to the deep and beefy character of the short ribs in this recipe. Fish sauce, an excellent complement to generously marbled meat, stands in for salt, so you don't need to salt. If you want to broil the ribs on the baking sheet in which they are drained and allowed to dry, be sure to line the pan with aluminum foil to avoid burnt-on caramelized juices.

½ cup (4 fl oz/125 ml) sake or dry white wine

¾ cup (6 fl oz/180 ml) reduced-sodium soy sauce

¼ cup (2 fl oz/60 ml) Thai or Vietnamese fish sauce

¼ cup (3 fl oz/90 g) honey

2 tablespoons peanut oil

1 teaspoon Asian sesame oil

7 large cloves garlic, minced

1 tablespoon peeled and minced fresh ginger

5 green onions, white and light green parts, minced

5 lb (2.5 kg) flanken-cut beef short ribs, cut ½ inch (12 mm) thick, patted dry

Freshly ground pepper

½ teaspoon five-spice powder

Combine the sake, soy sauce, fish sauce, honey, peanut oil, sesame oil, garlic, ginger, half of the green onions, and 1 cup (8 fl oz/250 ml) water in a large baking dish and mix well. Add the ribs to the dish and rub all sides of the ribs with the mixture. Let stand for at least 2 hours at room temperature or preferably overnight in the refrigerator, turning ribs once or twice.

Remove the ribs from the dish and discard the marinade. Place the ribs on a rack on a baking sheet. Let come to room temperature and air-dry for about 30 minutes.

Preheat the broiler. Season the ribs all over with about ¾ teaspoon pepper and the five-spice powder. Transfer the rack to a roasting pan. Place under the broiler about 3 inches (7.5 cm) from the heat source and cook the ribs, turning once, until nicely browned and sizzling on all sides, about 6 minutes per side.

Leave the ribs whole or, if desired, cut the ribs between the bones into smaller pieces. Garnish with the remaining green onions and serve at once.

### A NOTE FROM THE BUTCHER

Short ribs can be cut between the ribs (English cut) or across the ribs (flanken cut). Each slab of short ribs has a thick end, which has more meat, and a smaller end, which has less meat. Ask for your short ribs to be cut from the thick end and for the excess surface fat to be trimmed.

—Tanya Cauthen, Belmont Butchery, Richmond, VA

This is one of the most luxurious pieces of meat, often reserved for holiday dinners and other special occasions. Keep the roast loosely wrapped in butcher paper in the refrigerator until about 6½ hours before you plan to serve dinner (it takes 2 hours for the roast to come to room temperature). Leftovers, in the unlikely case there are any, can be turned into exceptional sandwiches: be sure to bring the meat to room temperature first.

Place the meat, fat side up, in a large roasting pan. Drape it with paper towels and let stand at room temperature for 2 hours. Cut 10 to 15 small slits all over the roast. Insert the garlic slivers in the slits far enough so they do not protrude above the surface.

Preheat the oven to 500°F (260°C). Let it preheat for about 30 minutes.

Brush the meat all over with the melted butter and season generously with salt. Insert an ovenproof meat thermometer into a cut side of the roast as close to the center as possible. Place the pan in the center of the oven. Roast for 7 minutes per pound (500 g) if using an electric oven, 6 minutes per pound if using a gas oven. Let the roast rest in the oven, without opening the door, for 2 hours. Note the internal temperature of the roast.

Sprinkle the top of the meat with a generous grinding of pepper and dust lightly with flour. Set the oven temperature to 500°F. Roast for 5–25 minutes, depending on the internal temperature you noted at the end of the resting period. If the internal temperature was 125°F (52°C), warm the meat for 15 minutes; if it was 115°F (46°C) or so, warm it for 20–25 minutes. If after 10 minutes the pan drippings smell as if they are burning, reduce the oven temperature to 450°F (230°C). Transfer the roast to a platter, tent loosely with aluminum foil, and let rest for 15 minutes.

Meanwhile, prepare the jus: In a small saucepan, combine the stock, parsley, and dill. Place over medium-low heat and warm just until the liquid is steaming. Taste and adjust the seasonings with salt and pepper.

Carve the roast crosswise between the bones (shown), for large, bone-in serving pieces. Or, cut the roast crosswise into thick or thin boneless slices, distributing the bones evenly among the plates. Serve at once, with the herbed jus on the side.

1 standing rib roast, 5 or 6 ribs, about 11 lb (5.5 kg), patted dry

4 large cloves garlic, cut into thin slivers

2 tablespoons salted butter, melted

Kosher salt and freshly ground pepper

Superfine flour for dusting

### FOR THE HERBED JUS

1¼ cups (10 fl oz/310 ml) rich homemade beef or veal stock or prepared consommé

2 teaspoons minced fresh flat-leaf parsley

2 teaspoons minced fresh dill

Kosher salt and freshly ground pepper

## BRAISED SHORT RIBS WITH ORANGE-TARRAGON CREAM

 MAKES 4–6 SERVINGS

Short ribs have a high collagen content, and slow, moist braising is the ideal way to transform this fibrous protein into a melt-in-your-mouth meat. A generous amount of wine in the braising liquid complements the meat and adds complexity to the reduced sauce. The ribs are especially good served over noodles or rice with plenty of their juices.

2 tablespoons olive oil

3½ lb (1.75 kg) bone-in short ribs

Kosher salt and freshly ground pepper

½ teaspoon fennel seeds, lightly crushed in a mortar

4 tablespoons (1 oz/30 g) all-purpose flour

2 oz (60 g) thick-sliced pancetta, cut into strips

1 large white or yellow onion, finely chopped

1 carrot, peeled and finely chopped

6 cloves garlic, smashed with the side of a heavy knife

1 tablespoon red wine vinegar

2½ cups (20 fl oz/625 ml) fruity red wine, such as Zinfandel

2 fresh thyme sprigs

2 bay leaves

⅔ cup (5 oz/155 g) canned crushed tomatoes, preferably San Marzano

1¾ cups (14 fl oz/430 ml) reduced-sodium beef or chicken broth

1 teaspoon minced fresh tarragon

Grated zest of 1 orange

¼ cup (2 oz/60 g) crème fraîche

Place a large Dutch oven or other heavy ovenproof pot over medium-high heat and add the oil. Season the ribs generously on all sides with salt and pepper. Dust with the fennel seeds and 2 tablespoons of the flour, shaking off the excess. When the oil is shimmering, add half of the ribs and sear until golden brown on all sides, about 10 minutes. Transfer to a platter and repeat with the remaining ribs.

Preheat the oven to 300°F (150°C).

Pour off most of the fat from the pot, leaving a thin film. Reduce the heat to medium and add the pancetta, onion, carrot, and garlic. Cook, stirring occasionally, until the vegetables have begun to brown, about 6 minutes. Sprinkle in the remaining 2 tablespoons flour, then stir and scrape the mixture constantly, until the flour is golden brown, about 2 minutes. If necessary, adjust the heat so the flour doesn't scorch. Stir in the vinegar and ½ cup (4 fl oz/125 ml) of the wine and deglaze the pot, stirring to scrape up browned bits from the bottom of the pot. Add the remaining wine, bring to a brisk simmer, and cook until the wine has reduced by about half, 8–10 minutes. Add the thyme, bay leaves, tomatoes, broth, ½ teaspoon salt, and plenty of pepper. Return the ribs to the pot, cover, and transfer to the oven. Cook until the meat is falling off the bones, turning the ribs about once an hour, about 3½ hours. Transfer the ribs to a platter.

Strain the braising liquid and vegetables through a fine-mesh sieve placed over a large heatproof bowl, scraping the vegetables back and forth to extract as much liquid as possible. Discard the solids. Let the liquid stand for 3–4 minutes, then skim off the fat from the top, if desired. Wipe out the pot, pour in the braising liquid, bring to a simmer over medium-high heat, and cook until slightly reduced, about 5 minutes.

Remove the bones and any chunks of fat or gristle from the short ribs. Cut the meat into bite-sized pieces. Return the meat to the pot and heat until warmed through, about 5 minutes.

Meanwhile, in a small bowl, stir together the tarragon, orange zest, and crème fraîche. Taste the braising liquid and adjust the seasonings. Serve at once, topped with the orange-tarragon cream.

Open the windows during the first hour or so of smoking the brisket so the smell doesn't linger. An instant-read thermometer—preferably a probe thermometer—is crucial here. Sometimes the temperature of the meat will stall at 155°F or 165°F (68°C or 74°C) for up to an hour. This is just a sign that the collagen is breaking down to create tender, juicy meat, so don't be tempted to increase the oven temperature.

Remove the racks from the oven and preheat it to 475°F (245°C). In a large aluminum foil roasting pan, thinly distribute 2 handfuls of dry oak or mesquite wood chips. On the chips, place a rack that will elevate a large baking dish for the meat at least 1 inch (2.5 cm) above the chips.

In a small bowl, stir together the mild chile powder, sugar, onion and garlic powders, mustard, hot-chile powder, 2 teaspoons salt, and 1 tablespoon pepper. Rub the brisket all over with the oil, then rub with spice mixture.

In the large baking dish, place a second, shallower rack. Set the dish on the rack in the foil roasting pan. Pour 1 cup (8 fl oz/250 ml) water into the baking dish. Place the meat, fat side up, on the rack. The water should not touch the meat.

Wrap both the roasting pan and the baking dish holding the meat with heavy-duty foil. Crimp the edges of the foil firmly so that it will hold in as much smoke as possible. Place directly on the floor of the oven and cook the meat for 35 minutes. Reduce the oven temperature to 225°F (110°C) and cook for 4 hours more.

Meanwhile, prepare the mop: In a small saucepan over medium heat, melt the butter. Stir in the vinegar and 3 tablespoons water.

Remove the foil from the pan and dish. Insert an ovenproof meat thermometer into the thickest part of the brisket. Brush the meat with the mop and continue to cook, brushing every 40 minutes or so, until the internal temperature reaches 190°F (88°C), 2–3 hours. If the temperature has not reached 190°F after a total cooking time of 7½ hours, raise the oven temperature to 300°F (150°C) and continue to cook the meat.

To the remaining mop, stir in the bourbon, honey, mustard, and ketchup. Turn on the broiler. Brush the meat with the bourbon-honey mixture. Broil, brushing the meat occasionally, until the top is crusty and dark brown, 5–15 minutes. Watch carefully to make sure that the meat does not char.

Remove the meat from the oven and let stand for 10 minutes. Cut into thick or thin slices and serve at once. The brisket can be wrapped in foil and held for up to 1½ hours.

# OVEN-SMOKED BRISKET WITH BOURBON-HONEY MOP

 MAKES 8–10 SERVINGS

1 teaspoon mild chile powder

1 teaspoon sugar

1 teaspoon onion powder

1 teaspoon garlic powder

1 teaspoon dry mustard

½ teaspoon hot chile powder

Kosher salt and freshly ground pepper

5 lb (2.5 kg) flat-cut brisket, lightly trimmed of excess fat

2 teaspoons canola oil

**FOR THE MOP**

3 tablespoons unsalted butter

3 tablespoons white vinegar

1 tablespoon bourbon

1 tablespoon honey

1 tablespoon Dijon mustard

1 tablespoon tomato ketchup

## ROASTED BEEF TENDERLOIN WITH MUSHROOM RAGOUT

 MAKES 6–8 SERVINGS

Tenderloin, a tender, special-occasion cut, is quite mild—not as beefy as rib roast. So here I add an earthy contrast of sherry-flavored woodsy mushrooms to serve alongside the meat. If you don't ask your butcher to trim the roast of silverskin, just make sure to snip through the sinewy layer every 3 to 4 inches (7.5 to 10 cm) to prevent the roast from curling. Serve hot or cold with Horseradish Crème Fraîche (page 213).

1 beef tenderloin, 3½–4 lb (1.75–2 kg), silverskin removed or snipped in several places

2 tablespoons whole-grain mustard

1½ tablespoons olive oil, plus more for searing

1½ teaspoons dried thyme

Kosher salt and freshly ground pepper

### FOR THE RAGOUT

2 tablespoons unsalted butter

2 large shallots, finely chopped

1 lb (500 g) mixed mushrooms, such as oyster and cremini, brushed clean and thickly sliced

¼ cup (2 fl oz/60 ml) Madeira or medium-dry sherry

¼ cup (2 fl oz/60 ml) heavy cream

2 teaspoons finely snipped fresh chives

Remove the tenderloin from the refrigerator and let stand at room temperature for 2 hours.

Preheat the oven to 425°F (220°C).

Whisk together the mustard, 1½ tablespoons oil, and the thyme. Set aside. Using kitchen string, tie the tenderloin firmly at 1½-inch (4-cm) intervals, to keep it plump and round during cooking. Pat thoroughly dry and season all sides generously with salt. Heat a large roasting pan over medium-high heat until it is very hot, about 3 minutes. Add enough oil to the pan to coat the bottom. When the oil is shimmering, add the tenderloin and sear without moving for 2½ minutes. Turn and continue to sear until the tenderloin has an even, dark brown crust on all sides. Transfer to a cutting board, brush with the mustard mixture, and season generously with pepper.

Set a rack in the roasting pan and transfer the tenderloin to the rack. Place in the oven and cook until an instant-read thermometer inserted into the center of the roast registers 125°–130°F (52°–54°C), 15–20 minutes. The temperature will range from rare to medium-rare in different parts of the tenderloin. Transfer the tenderloin to a platter, tent loosely with aluminum foil, and let rest for at least 15 minutes or up to 30 minutes.

While the meat is resting, prepare the ragout: In a large frying pan over medium heat, melt the butter. Add the shallots and cook until softened, about 5 minutes. Add the mushrooms and cook, stirring occasionally, until they release their liquid, about 10 minutes. Add the Madeira and simmer until almost completely evaporated. Stir in the cream, chives, ¼ teaspoon salt, and pepper to taste. Continue to cook, stirring, until the ragout is thick, creamy, and bubbling, 1–2 minutes more.

Snip the strings and cut the tenderloin into slices about ½ inch (12 mm) thick. Arrange on plates with the ragout. Serve at once.

### A NOTE FROM THE BUTCHER

Purchase a whole 6- to 7-pound (3- to 3.5-kg) tenderloin; it is a better value than a center-cut roast. Ask your butcher to prepare it "chef ready," with the gristly side muscle and the silverskin removed and the roast tied.

—Michael Milazo, Alexander's Prime Meats and Catering, San Gabriel, CA

This dish, which uses Syrah wine (called Shiraz in Australia) as the braising liquid, is a friendlier-on-the-budget version of braised beef in Barolo, an Italian classic. The flavors develop and intensify as the meat stands in the rich braising juices, so prepare it 1–2 days in advance, cover, and refrigerate. Rewarm the meat and sauce gently over medium-low heat. Serve as is with crusty bread for soaking up the juices, or serve over polenta or steamed rice.

## BRAISED BEEF IN RED WINE

 MAKES 6 SERVINGS

In a small bowl, stir together the parsley, rosemary, sage, and garlic. Set aside. Cut slits about ¼ inch (6 mm) deep all over the brisket. Push a strip of bacon into each slit. On a large plate, stir together the ⅓ cup flour, the paprika, 1 teaspoon salt, and ½ teaspoon pepper. Dredge the brisket in the flour mixture, shaking off the excess.

In a large Dutch oven or other heavy, ovenproof pot over medium-low heat, melt the butter with the oil. Add the onion and cook until softened, 3–4 minutes. Raise the heat to medium-high and push the onion to one side. Add the brisket and scatter the garlic-herb mixture, bay leaves, carrots, and celery around the edges of the pot. Cook the brisket, turning, until browned on all sides. Stir the herbs and vegetables as needed to prevent them from scorching. Transfer the meat to a platter and preheat the oven to 300°F (150°C).

Drain off any excess fat from the vegetable-herb mixture. Sprinkle with the remaining 2 tablespoons flour and stir to incorporate. Add 1 cup (8 fl oz/250 ml) of the wine. Place over medium-high heat and bring to a boil. Cook, stirring occasionally, until the liquid is reduced by half. Add the remaining 2 cups (16 fl oz/500 ml) wine and season with salt and pepper. Bring to a simmer and return the brisket to the pot. Cover, place in the oven, and cook, turning the meat every 45 minutes, until fork-tender, 4–5 hours.

Transfer the brisket to a platter. Taste the sauce and adjust the seasoning if necessary. Pour over the brisket and serve at once.

3 tablespoons minced fresh
flat-leaf parsley

2 tablespoons minced fresh rosemary

2 teaspoons minced fresh sage

4 cloves garlic, minced

3 lb (1.5 kg) flat-cut beef brisket,
trimmed of excess fat

3 slices lean bacon, cut crosswise
into strips ¼ inch (6 mm) wide

⅓ cup (2 oz/60 g) all-purpose flour
plus 2 tablespoons

1 teaspoon sweet paprika

Kosher salt and freshly ground pepper

2 tablespoons unsalted butter

1 tablespoon olive oil

1 small yellow onion, thinly sliced

2 bay leaves

2 carrots, peeled and diced

2 ribs celery, diced

3 cups (24 fl oz/750 ml) full-bodied
red wine, such as Syrah or Shiraz

There's nothing like high heat to dry out an innocent pork chop. Don't use searingly hot heat and your chops will be extremely flavorful. Our rule is the thicker the cut, the lower the temperature. A good butcher will know how thick to cut your chops if you describe your recipe.

—Otto Demke, Gepperth's Meat Market, Chicago, IL

# PORK

# PORK
## PRIMER

In the United States, pork is not as intensively graded as beef. In the absence of grades, knowing how to identify high-quality meat is very important. The most crucial attribute to recognize in pork is the extent of the marbling. This will be your primary clue as to how tasty the meat will be. But don't be afraid to ask your butcher questions: How was the pig raised? Was it allowed to roam free in a pasture? Was its diet mostly grass and wild forage, or was it fed grain? If you know such essential information, you can make the best choice for the recipe you are preparing.

### CONVENTIONAL PORK VS. HEIRLOOM BREEDS

Worldwide, pork is the most popular meat on the table, but in the United States, consumers' avoidance of pork due to a concern for dietary fat prompted producers to breed leaner pigs. They fed the animals a restricted diet and confined them to feedlots. Because of this market-driven trend toward leaner meat lacking intramuscular fat, some of the qualities appreciated in traditional pork were lost. Lean pork has little flavor, and the lack of marbling can make it dry and chewy after cooking. Heirloom breeds such as Berkshire, Duroc, and Yorkshire have become more widely available. Due to the pigs' varied diet, their meat is rich tasting, juicy, and tender.

### IDENTIFYING FRESH PORK

Pork ranges in color from very pale pink to a rosy hue. In general, the more color, the better the flavor. Pale pork, a sign of poor quality, signals that the meat will lack flavor and dry out easily. The marbling and exterior fat should be perfectly white, never yellow, and the surface of the meat should be springy and moist, not wet. When it comes to freshness, let your nose be your guide. Ask your butcher to let you examine the cut you need. If purchasing wrapped meat, check the sell-by date. When you get home, unwrap the meat and check the smell: if it smells off, return it to the store.

### SAFETY

Fear of trichinosis, caused by a parasite, once dictated that pork be cooked to an internal temperature of 160°F (71°C). Trichinosis is actually killed at 137°F (58°C), and therefore the widely accepted doneness temperature for pork is now 145°F (63°C). Well-marbled cuts such as the shoulder will maintain their juiciness when slowly cooked to a higher temperature, but leaner cuts such as the loin will dry out quickly when cooked above 145°F.

## PORK AT A GLANCE

**Look for** pinkish red, well-marbled meat with a moist but not wet surface.

**Avoid** pale, soft meat.

**Cuts to remember** rack of pork, scallops, shanks.

**Best value** shoulder.

**Splurge cuts** bone-in belly roast, center-cut loin chops.

**Best cut to grind for burgers** shoulder.

**Storage** 3 days in the refrigerator; up to 6 months in the freezer.

## BEST FLAVORS FOR PORK

**American flavors** garlic, onions, lemon, orange, mustard, maple syrup, fresh and dried fruits.

**Asian flavors** ginger, soy, lemongrass, rice vinegar.

**Mediterranean flavors** tomatoes, figs, olives, capers, oregano, cured pork (prosciutto, pancetta, chorizo), wine, balsamic vinegar.

**Latin flavors** lime, chiles, cilantro, mangoes.

## PORK BASICS

**TRIMMING** Fat carries flavor and acts as a natural basting agent to keep the meat moist, especially on leaner cuts such as loin and tenderloin. Therefore, you want to remove only the excess fat. The exterior fat on larger cuts such as the shoulder can be trimmed slightly, but preferably not to less than ⅛ or ¼ inch (6 or 12 mm). When you purchase pork, you can request that your butcher trim the meat to your specification as well as remove silverskin from a tenderloin or tie a roast for you.

**BRINGING TO ROOM TEMPERATURE** The cooking times for the recipes in this book are based on room-temperature meat. The time required to bring refrigerated meat to room temperature depends on the cut. A pork chop that is ½ inch (12 mm) thick may take only 15 minutes and a tenderloin 30 minutes, whereas a shoulder or loin may need 1 to 2 hours. If a cut of meat, especially a large one, is cooked while still cold, it will take longer to reach the proper internal temperature.

**SEASONING** The choice of seasonings should be influenced by the cut of pork and how it will be cooked. Chops, cutlets, and medallions sliced from tenderloin need only a sprinkling of salt and pepper before being panfried. Chops, loin, and other cuts take well to an overnight soaking in a brine enhanced with various seasonings. Stuffing chops or a loin offers a way to season the meat from the inside out. When the meat will be seared or panfried, it should be patted dry with paper towels to remove any moisture that will inhibit browning.

**RESTING** Resting pork after cooking allows the juices to settle and redistribute. The resting period can range from about 5 minutes for a chop to 30 minutes for a shoulder.

**STORING** Pork that is pre-wrapped in plastic from the supermarket should be consumed within 2 days. If you want to keep it for a day or so longer, it's best to rewrap the meat in breathable butcher's paper. Cuts that are vacuum sealed may be kept longer, following the recommendation on the package (be sure to rinse well before using). Well-marbled cuts like shoulder and butt take better to freezing than the leaner cuts like leg, loin, and tenderloin. First wrap the meat tightly in plastic wrap, then enclose it with aluminum foil, sealing the seams securely. It can be frozen for up to 6 months. The safest way to defrost frozen pork is to transfer it to the refrigerator about 3 days before you plan to cook it. Never try to rush the thawing process by heating the pork in a microwave or with hot water; the exterior will begin to cook while the center will remain frozen.

## FAQS FOR THE BUTCHER

Q: What is the difference between the pork I see at the farmer's market and the pork I buy at the supermarket?

A: A lot! What you're paying for at the farmer's market is generally a pig that has been raised outside on pasture and has been fed a wide variety of foods, including wild forage. This results in more fat and more flavor. Typical grocery-store pork is raised indoors and fed grain only. This results in leaner, less flavorful pork.

Q: What cuts offer the best value?

A: Sirloin and shoulder chops are great for grilling. These cuts are tender if cooked over moderate heat, and offer more flavor for less money than, say, center-cut pork chops. For slow cooking, try neck and shank, which have the most pronounced "porky" flavor.

Q: I bought a pork roast that still has the skin on it. Should I remove it before cooking it?

A: Please don't! There are few things as delicious as crispy pork skin or "crackling" as it is sometimes called. To ensure that the fat renders properly, slit the skin all over to a depth of about ¼ inch (6 mm).

— Tom Mylan, The Meat Hook, Brooklyn, NY

## COOKING BY THE CUT

**Best for panfrying** scallops; center-cut rib chops; loin chops; tenderloin medallions; ham steak.

**Best for grilling** rib, sirloin, and loin chops; spareribs; tenderloin (kebabs); belly; shoulder (burgers).

**Best for roasting** bone-in or boneless loin, rack, ham/leg, bone-in belly, tenderloin; lean cuts can quickly cook in the high, dry heat of the oven.

**Best for braising** cuts with generous marbling, such as shoulder, shank, country-style ribs, bone-in or boneless belly, picnic ham/shoulder, shoulder blade chops.

## TAKE THE TEMPERATURE

Today it is common practice to serve pork slightly pink at the center. Pork is never served rare.

**Cutlets and scallops** too thin to measure the temperature; should feel just firm to the touch.

**Chops and lean roasts (loin, rack of ribs, tenderloin, leg)** remove from the heat at 140° (60°C); ideal temperature after resting: 145°F (63°C).

**Well-marbled pork roasts (shoulder, picnic ham, belly, shank)** follow the recipe guidelines, but remove from the heat between 155° and 190°F (68° and 88°C).

**Ribs** done when tender but not falling off the bone. Twist the tip of a bone near the center of the rack; if it starts to break free of the meat, the ribs are done.

## THE CUTS

When butchered, a pig is usually divided into four large sections, as shown at right and listed below, which are then divided into cuts suitable for cooking. Similar to other animals, the muscles of the pig that work the hardest—the shoulder and the rear legs (ham)—produce tougher meat than the more sedentary parts, such as the belly and loin, which produce the most tender, highly marbled cuts.

**SHOULDER** Cuts from the shoulder contain a lot of marbling, which gives the meat a deep, rich flavor and makes the shoulder more forgiving when cooked. Shoulder cuts also contain a relatively high proportion of collagen, or connective tissue. This could make the meat tough, but when the proper cooking method is used, the collagen melts and the resulting meat is tasty and tender. The top of the shoulder, also called Boston butt, is often braised—a foolproof way to render the meat delicious. Picnic ham, from the bottom of the shoulder, can be roasted very slowly or braised with great success.

**LOIN** The loin is the source of loin chops with their T-shaped bone and rib chops with their small rib bones. Chops from the shoulder end, also called blade chops, carry a bit more marbling; center-cut and loin-end chops are leaner. The loin itself, whether bone-in or boneless, makes a superb roast. A rack of pork chops is a luxury cut, all the more impressive if roasted with a stuffing in the center. Back ribs and spare ribs are high in collagen and therefore best suited to moist, low-heat cooking.

**HAM/LEG** A whole roasted leg, whether fresh or cured (ham), is an economical choice for feeding a crowd. For smaller gatherings, use half a ham from the butt end, and always choose a bone-in ham for juicier, tastier results. Meat from the leg is lean, just like the loin, so roasting is the best cooking method. Thick ham steaks can also be pan roasted. Shanks contain lots of collagen and are most often cured and/or smoked; large shanks are delicious braised.

**BELLY** Fresh belly has recently gained in popularity and now graces the menus of even upscale restaurants. Many people do not realize they have long been eating cured pork belly in the form of bacon. With this cut, the fat and skin are as important as the meat. A thick piece of bone-in belly with skin makes an excellent roast. Boneless belly with its skin can be grilled, and bone-in or boneless belly with or without its skin braises well.

# PORK CHART

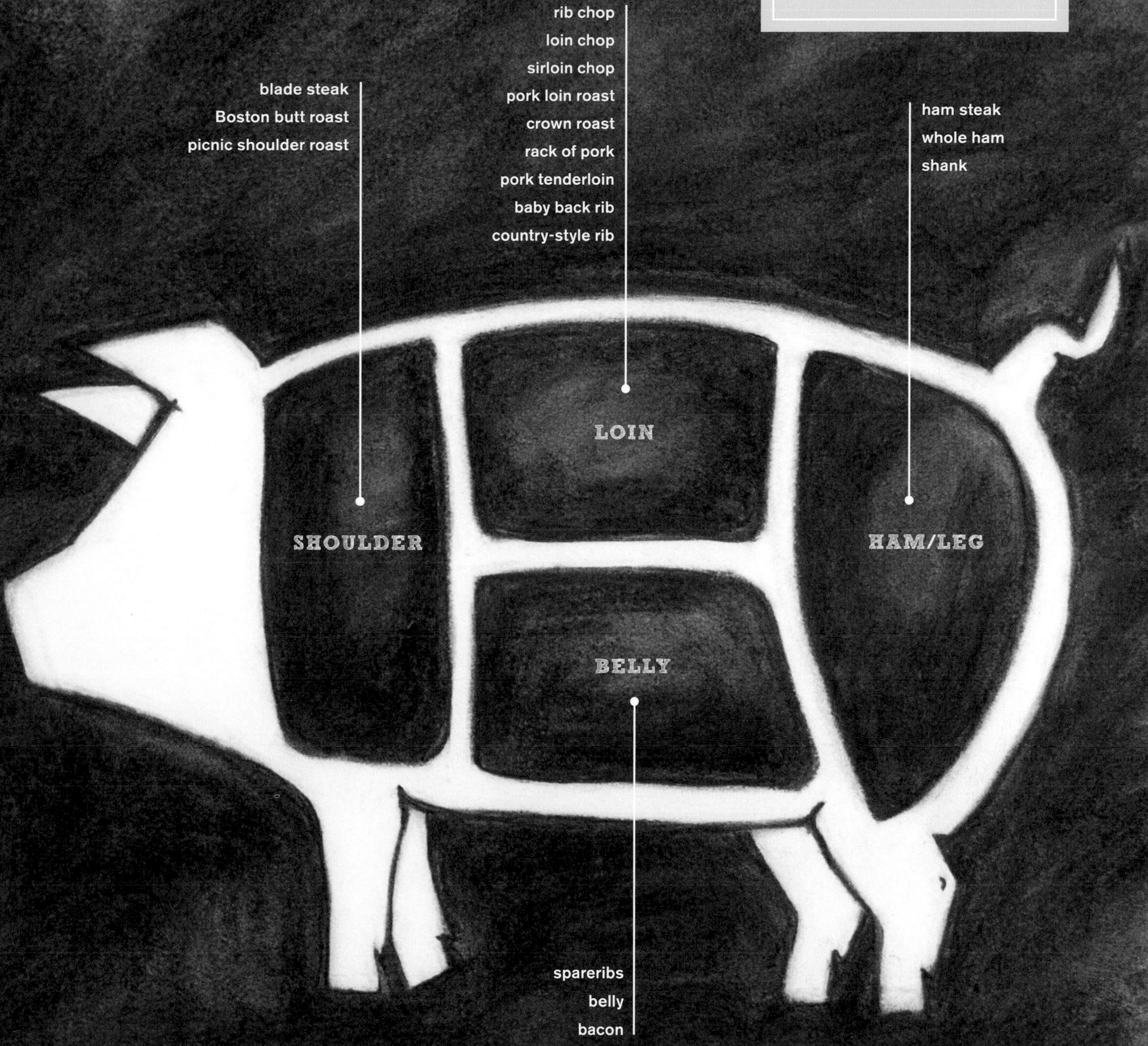

blade steak
Boston butt roast
picnic shoulder roast
rib chop
loin chop
sirloin chop
pork loin roast
crown roast
rack of pork
pork tenderloin
baby back rib
country-style rib
ham steak
whole ham
shank
LOIN
SHOULDER
HAM/LEG
BELLY
spareribs
belly
bacon

**MAKES 4 SERVINGS**

Quick cooking and loaded with flavor, this is the perfect dish for a weeknight supper. I like to cut the eggplant into thick matchsticks so that as much of the flesh is exposed to the high heat as possible. The pieces will brown on the outside, but not turn mushy or soggy on the inside. If you don't have a large frying pan or wok, cook the pork in batches to avoid overcrowding the pan.

Place the pork on a baking sheet and freeze, uncovered, for 15 minutes. Cut the pork into strips about 2 inches (5 cm) long, ¾ inch (2 cm) wide, and ½ inch (12 mm) thick. Season generously with salt and pepper. Cut the eggplant into strips of the same size.

In a small bowl, whisk together the chile paste, sesame oil, and vinegar until smooth. Set aside.

Heat 2 tablespoons of the peanut oil in a large frying pan or wok over high heat until very hot, 2–3 minutes. Add the eggplant and toss and stir every 15–20 seconds until slightly softened, 3–4 minutes. Add the ginger and the green onion pieces and toss and stir for 1 minute more. Scrape the vegetables onto a platter.

Add the remaining 1 tablespoon peanut oil to the pan and swirl to coat. When the oil is very hot, add the pork, distributing it evenly, and cook without moving it for about 20 seconds. With a metal spatula, toss and stir the pork every 15–20 seconds until browned, about 3 minutes more.

Return the vegetables to the pan and add the chile paste mixture. Reduce the heat to medium and toss and stir for 1–2 minutes to blend the flavors and warm through. Scatter with the chopped green onions and serve at once.

1 pork tenderloin, about 1 lb (500 g), silverskin removed and trimmed of excess fat

Kosher salt and freshly ground pepper

1 small globe eggplant, about 1 lb (500 g)

2 tablespoons chile paste with garlic

1½ teaspoons Asian sesame oil

1½ teaspoons rice vinegar

3 tablespoons peanut or canola oil

1 tablespoon peeled and minced fresh ginger

6 green onions, white and light green parts, 4 halved lengthwise and cut into ¾-inch (2-cm) pieces, 2 finely chopped

# PANFRIED PORK CHOPS WITH PICKLED RED ONIONS AND THYME

 MAKES 4 SERVINGS

For particularly juicy results, brine the chops for 2 to 6 hours (see page 90), but if so, don't season them with salt before cooking. If using chops thicker than ¾ inch (2 cm), add 30 seconds extra cooking time per side for every ¼ inch (6 mm). Avoid buying chops thicker than 1¼ inches (3 cm); these are better suited to a two-part cooking process, as for the grilled stuffed chops on page 106.

**FOR THE PICKLED RED ONIONS**

1 cup (8 fl oz/250 ml) red wine vinegar

1 cup (8 fl oz/250 ml) dry red wine

½ cup (4 oz/125 g) sugar

1 tablespoon yellow mustard seeds

2 tablespoons black peppercorns

2 teaspoons red pepper flakes

Kosher salt

2 small or 1 large red onion, cut crosswise into rings ¼ inch (6 mm) thick

4 bone-in pork rib chops, each about 7 oz (220 g) and ¾ inch (2 cm) thick

Kosher salt and freshly ground pepper

1½ tablespoons olive oil

2 small fresh thyme sprigs

½ teaspoon minced fresh thyme

To make the pickled onion, in a saucepan over low heat, combine the vinegar, wine, sugar, mustard seeds, peppercorns, red pepper flakes, and 2 tablespoons salt. Stir until the sugar and salt have dissolved. Add the onion rings, bring the liquid to a boil, and then lower the heat and simmer for about 5 minutes. Let cool completely before serving. Alternatively, transfer the hot onion and liquid to a sterilized jar, cover tightly, and refrigerate. Bring to room temperature before serving.

Remove the pork from the refrigerator, pat the chops dry, and let stand at room temperature for 30 minutes. Season both sides generously with salt and pepper.

Preheat the oven to 170°F (75°C) and place a platter in the oven to warm.

Place a large frying pan over medium-high heat and add half of the oil and the thyme sprigs. When the oil is shimmering, add 2 chops and sear without moving them for 2½ minutes. Turn and cook until golden and firm to the touch, about 2½ minutes more. Transfer the chops to the platter and keep warm in the oven. Repeat with the remaining oil and the remaining chops.

Arrange the chops on plates and top with the pickled onion. Garnish with minced thyme and serve at once.

---

**A NOTE FROM THE BUTCHER**

There's nothing like high heat to dry out an innocent pork chop. Don't use searingly hot heat and your chops will be extremely flavorful. Our rule is the thicker the cut, the lower the temperature. A good butcher will know how thick to cut your chops if you describe your recipe.

—Otto Demke, Gepperth's Meat Market, Chicago, IL

---

This substantial sandwich is loaded with big flavors from the fig jam, mustard, and radicchio-carrot slaw. The use of mustard and fig may sound surprising, but the two add sweetness with a little zing. The pork cutlets called for here are thicker than scallops, but both cuts are sometimes referred to as "scallops." If you don't see cutlets on display, ask your butcher to cut slices ¾ inch (2 cm) thick from the loin.

## PORK LOIN SANDWICHES WITH RADICCHIO-CARROT SLAW

MAKES 6 SERVINGS

To make the slaw, in a bowl, combine the radicchio and carrot. Fold in the oil, then add the vinegar and parsley. Add ½ teaspoon salt and season with pepper. Taste and adjust the seasoning. If desired, stir in a little sugar.

Generously season both sides of the cutlets with salt and pepper. Place a large, heavy frying pan over medium-high heat and add the oil. When the oil is shimmering, place the cutlets in the pan without letting them touch and cook without moving them until golden brown, about 3 minutes. Turn and cook until golden, about 3 minutes more. Reduce the heat to very low and continue to cook the cutlets, turning them once, until springy to the touch, about 5 minutes. Transfer to a cutting board and let rest, uncovered, for 5–10 minutes. Cut the pork on a very steep diagonal into slices about ¼ inch (6 mm) thick.

Spread 1 tablespoon of the fig jam on each of 6 bread slices. Spread the mustard on the remaining 6 slices. Divide the pork among the jam-covered slices, then top with the slaw and the remaining bread slices. Serve at once.

### FOR THE RADICCHIO-CARROT SLAW

2 cups (6 oz/185 g) shredded radicchio

¾ cup (4 oz/125 g) shredded carrot

3 tablespoons extra-virgin olive oil

2 tablespoons white wine vinegar

1 tablespoon coarsely chopped fresh flat-leaf parsley

Kosher salt and freshly ground pepper

¼–½ teaspoon sugar (optional)

3 pork cutlets from loin or leg, each about 6 by 3 inches (15 by 7.5 cm) and ¾ inch (2 cm) thick

Kosher salt and freshly ground pepper

1 tablespoon olive oil

6 tablespoons (3 oz/90 g) fig jam or preserves

12 slices coarse country bread, each about ⅓ inch (9 mm) thick

3 tablespoons Dijon mustard, or to taste

---

### ⬛ A NOTE FROM THE BUTCHER

Let the pork cutlets come to room temperature before cooking. Be sure to panfry the pork gently and monitor it carefully; it can overcook quickly. Remember, too, that the meat will continue to cook once it is removed from the heat.

—Mark Cacioppo, Ottomanelli Brothers, New York, NY

# PANFRIED PORK LOIN CHOPS WITH MUSTARD-CAPER SAUCE

**MAKES 4 SERVINGS**

Supermarket pork chops benefit greatly from being submerged in a simple brine. Make enough brine to cover the chops, usually 4 to 8 cups (32 to 64 fl oz/1 to 2 l), and use a ratio of ¼ cup (2 oz/60 g) kosher salt per 4 cups water. Add a few bay leaves and some peppercorns, and refrigerate the chops for 6 hours. At least 30 minutes before you plan to cook the chops, remove them from the brine, rinse, and then dry thoroughly with paper towels.

4 center-cut pork loin chops, each about 7 oz (220 g) and ¾ inch (2 cm) thick

Kosher salt and freshly ground pepper

1½ tablespoons olive oil

⅓ cup (2½ oz/75 g) capers

1¼ cups (10 fl oz/310 ml) vermouth or semidry white wine

⅓ cup (3 fl oz/80 ml) heavy cream

¼ teaspoon white wine vinegar

2 tablespoons whole-grain mustard

Remove the pork from the refrigerator and let stand for 30 minutes. Pat the chops dry and season both sides generously with salt and pepper.

Preheat the oven to 170°F (75°C) and place a platter in the oven to warm.

Place a large frying pan over high heat and add half of the oil. When the oil has begun to shimmer, reduce the heat to medium-high, add 2 chops, and sear without moving them for 2½ minutes. Turn and cook until golden and firm to the touch but still have a little give, about 2½ minutes more. Transfer the chops to the platter and keep warm in the oven. Repeat with the remaining oil and the remaining chops.

Pour any oil from the pan. Reduce the heat to medium and add the capers to the pan. Cook for 1 minute. Add the vermouth, bring to a simmer, and cook until reduced by about half, about 2 minutes. Stir in the cream, vinegar, and ¼ teaspoon salt and season with pepper. Simmer the sauce until lightly thickened, about 30 seconds. Remove from the heat and whisk in the mustard. Taste and adjust the seasoning.

Pour some of the sauce over the chops on the platter. Serve at once, passing the remaining sauce at the table.

---

### A NOTE FROM THE BUTCHER

When selecting pork chops, pick those that have a darker, richer color. They will have a more pronounced pork flavor and be juicier than pale-colored chops. Don't forget that pork is meant to be enjoyed medium-rare. It is completely safe to eat when it reaches a temperature of 137°F (58°C), although as it rests, it should reach 145° to 150°F (63° to 65°C), the perfect serving temperature.

—Mark Martin, Nelson's Meat Market, Cedar Rapids, IA

---

Pork tenderloin, especially from today's leaner pigs, is tender but notoriously difficult to keep moist during cooking. To combat this, I use a two-pronged approach: I cook the pork briefly and then introduce richness by finishing with a drizzle of herb oil. If you have leftover herb oil, let it stand overnight; the next day, strain out the herbs. You can store the oil in the refrigerator for up to 2 weeks.

To make the herb oil, bring a small saucepan of water to a boil. Add the basil and tarragon, stir once to immerse, and cook until bright green and wilted, about 45 seconds. Drain in a colander and immediately rinse under cool running water to stop the cooking. Squeeze the herbs in a towel to extract as much water as possible. In a mini food processor, combine the herbs and oil. Pulse several times to blend thoroughly, scraping down the sides of the bowl as needed.

Preheat the oven to 170°F (75°C) and place a platter in the oven to warm.

Place the pork medallions between sheets of plastic wrap and, using the flat side of a meat mallet, pound to an even thickness of about 1¼ inches (3 cm). Rub both sides with a little oil. Let stand at room temperature for 15 minutes. Season both sides lightly with salt and pepper.

Place a large frying pan over medium-high heat and add the 1 tablespoon oil. When the oil is shimmering, add the medallions without letting them touch and sear without moving them for 2 minutes. Turn and cook for 1 minute more. Reduce the heat to very low and continue to cook, turning once, until just firm to the touch, about 1½ minutes per side. Transfer the medallions to the platter and keep warm in the oven.

Pour off any oil from the pan. Place over medium-low heat and add the butter. As soon as it melts, add the shallot and bell pepper and cook, stirring, until the pepper is slightly softened, about 3 minutes. Add the zucchini, yellow squash, and ½–¾ teaspoon salt and season with pepper. Cook for 3 minutes. Add the corn and cook, stirring occasionally, until the vegetables are tender but not mushy, about 2 minutes more. Taste and adjust the seasoning.

Arrange the medallions and vegetables on plates. Drizzle generously with the herb oil and serve at once.

# PAN-ROASTED PORK MEDALLIONS WITH SUMMER VEGETABLES

**MAKES 4 SERVINGS**

**FOR THE HERB OIL**

¼ cup (¼ oz/7 g) loosely packed fresh basil leaves

¼ cup (¼ oz/7 g) loosely packed fresh tarragon leaves

⅔ cup (5 fl oz/160 ml) extra-virgin olive oil

1 pork tenderloin, about 1½ lb (750 g), silverskin removed, trimmed of excess fat, and cut crosswise into 8 medallions

1 tablespoon olive oil, plus more for rubbing

Kosher salt and freshly ground pepper

2 tablespoons unsalted butter

1 large shallot, minced

1 large red, orange, or yellow bell pepper, seeded and diced

2 small zucchini, cut into slices about ⅛ inch (3 mm) thick

1 yellow squash, cut into slices about ⅛ inch (3 mm) thick

1 cup (6 oz/185 g) corn kernels (from about 2 small ears)

## PORK SCALOPPINE WITH PROSCIUTTO AND CAPERS

**MAKES 4 SERVINGS**

I rarely pass up the chance to pair the intense, complex flavor of cured pork with fresh pork—and this recipe shows off that winning combination. If your pan isn't big enough to cook all the cutlets in one layer, cook them in two batches or use two pans. Don't move the cutlets after placing them in the pan until it is time to turn them, as they need to develop a perfectly golden crust.

½ cup (2½ oz/75 g) all-purpose flour

Kosher salt and freshly ground pepper

2 tablespoons olive oil

4 pork cutlets from loin or leg, each about 6 by 3 inches (15 by 7.5 cm) and ¾ inch (2 cm) thick

3 oz (90 g) thinly sliced prosciutto, coarsely chopped

2 cloves garlic, minced

3 tablespoons capers

1½ cups (12 fl oz/375 ml) dry white wine or vermouth

2 or 3 anchovy fillets, rinsed and patted dry (optional)

Grated zest of 1 lemon

1 tablespoon coarsely chopped fresh flat-leaf parsley, dill, or chervil

On a plate, combine the flour and ¾ teaspoon salt. Season with pepper. Place a large, heavy frying pan over medium-high heat and add the olive oil. When the oil has begun to shimmer, quickly dredge both sides of the cutlets in the seasoned flour, shaking off the excess. Place the cutlets in the pan without letting them touch and cook without moving them until golden brown, about 3 minutes. Turn and cook until golden, 2–3 minutes more. Transfer to a platter.

Reduce the heat to medium and quickly add the prosciutto, garlic, and capers. Cook, stirring frequently, until the prosciutto is lightly golden, about 2 minutes. Stir in the wine, anchovies (if using), and lemon zest. Return the cutlets to the pan and cook until the liquid is reduced by about half and the cutlets are cooked through but not dry, 5–6 minutes. Taste and adjust the seasoning, adding salt if not using anchovies.

Garnish with the parsley and serve at once.

In autumn, when the light changes and there's a briskness in the air, this is my go-to dish for a satisfying meal at home. Adding just a small quantity of maple syrup to the brine gives the meat a hint of sweetness, which shines through when the pork is paired with the sweet-and-savory pear chutney (which can be prepared up to 5 days ahead). I like to pour an Oregon Pinot Noir with this dish.

To prepare the chutney, combine the pears and vinegar in a small saucepan over low heat. Cook, stirring frequently to prevent scorching, until the pears begin to break down, about 15 minutes. Remove from the heat and add the brown sugar, stirring until it has dissolved. Add the ginger and return to low heat. Cook, stirring almost constantly, until the mixture is dark brown and very thick, about 10 minutes. Let cool to room temperature, then cover and refrigerate. The chutney will keep for up to 5 days.

In a tall, narrow nonreactive container that will fit in your refrigerator, combine 2½ qt (2.5 l) cold water and the salt, maple syrup, bay leaves, and peppercorns. Stir until the salt dissolves. Submerge the chops in the brine. Refrigerate for at least 6 hours or up to overnight.

Remove the chops from the brine and discard the brine. Rinse the chops, then pat thoroughly dry, and let stand on a rack to dry further, about 10 minutes.

Heat a large cast-iron pan over medium-high heat until very hot, about 3 minutes. Brush both sides of the chops lightly with oil and season generously with pepper. Add the chops to the pan without letting them touch and cook without moving them for 2 minutes. Turn and cook for 2 minutes more. Reduce the heat to very low and continue cooking the chops, turning once, until an instant-read thermometer inserted into the center of a chop away from the bone registers 140°F (60°C), about 6 minutes per side. Transfer to a platter and let rest for 3–5 minutes.

Arrange the chops on plates and serve at once with the chutney.

# MAPLE-BRINED PORK CHOPS WITH PEAR CHUTNEY

 | MAKES 6 SERVINGS

**FOR THE PEAR CHUTNEY**

3 large, firm pears, such as Bartlett, Bosc, or Comice, peeled, quartered, cored, and coarsely chopped

1½ tablespoons white wine vinegar

⅔ cup (5 oz/155 g) firmly packed golden brown sugar

1¼ tablespoons peeled and minced fresh ginger

⅔ cup (5½ oz/170 g) kosher salt

½ cup (5½ oz/170 g) maple syrup

2 bay leaves, crumbled

2 tablespoons peppercorns

6 bone-in pork loin chops, each about ½ lb (250 g) and ¾ inch (2 cm) thick

Olive oil for brushing

Freshly ground pepper

---

**A NOTE FROM THE BUTCHER**

You can add extra flavor and tenderness by injecting some of the brine into the meat with a stitch pump, a syringe-type instrument commonly used for preserving meats. For a flavorful garnish, make an aioli with rendered pork fat instead of oil.

—Kristin Tombers, Clancey's Meats and Fish, Minneapolis, MN

---

## SMOKED PORK CHOPS WITH SUMMER SUCCOTASH

 MAKES 4 SERVINGS

Smoked pork chops vary in size and thickness. Ideally, for this recipe, buy smoked pork chops from your butcher's cold case. These bone-in, meaty chops are large and satisfying. If you use the small boneless chops found in the smoked-meats section of your supermarket, they will require only half the time for searing.

2 tablespoons unsalted butter

½ cup (2½ oz/75 g) finely chopped yellow onion

2½ cups (15 oz/470 g) corn kernels (from about 4 ears)

1 cup (5 oz/155 g) fresh or thawed frozen baby lima beans

½ cup (4 fl oz/125 ml) heavy cream

Kosher salt and freshly ground pepper

3 small plum tomatoes, seeded and diced (optional)

1 tablespoon canola oil

4 bone-in smoked pork chops, about 1 inch (2.5 cm) thick

1–2 teaspoons fresh lemon juice

In a large frying pan over medium-low heat, melt the butter. Add the onion and cook, stirring, until translucent, 8–10 minutes. Add the corn, lima beans, and cream and season with salt and pepper. Cook, stirring frequently, until the mixture thickens slightly, 10–15 minutes. Stir in the tomatoes, if using. Remove from the heat.

While the succotash is cooking, remove the pork from the refrigerator and let stand for 30 minutes.

Place a large, heavy frying pan over medium-high heat and add the oil. When the oil begins to shimmer, season both sides of the chops with pepper. Add the chops to the pan without letting them touch and cook, turning once, until golden, about 2½ minutes per side. Reduce the heat to very low and continue to cook the chops until they are no longer red in the center and an instant-read thermometer inserted into the center of a chop away from the bone registers 140°F (60°C), 2–7 minutes. Transfer to a platter and let rest, loosely covered with aluminum foil, for 3–5 minutes.

Taste the succotash and adjust the seasoning. Stir in 1 teaspoon of the lemon juice or more to taste. Reheat if necessary. Arrange the chops and succotash on plates and serve at once.

---

### A NOTE FROM THE BUTCHER

Smoked pork chops are just like ham on a bone. They are purchased fully cooked and seasoned, so they do not need added salt and just need to be warmed up to be ready for serving. The end cut of a smoked loin is the perfect addition to pea soup or baked beans.

—Otto Demke, Gepperth's Meat Market, Chicago, IL

---

These skewers have it all: bacon, which bastes the tender, lean pork; bread cubes, which turn into crisp, brown croutons; and sage leaves, which season the bread and meat as they cook on the grill. Serve the kebabs on their own, or over a simply dressed green salad—romaine or iceberg is sturdy enough to stand up to the heat of the skewers—and accompany with a nutty amber ale.

Cut the tenderloin into 1-inch (2-cm) cubes. You will need about 20 cubes. Reserve any remaining pork for another use. If using bamboo skewers, soak 4 long skewers in water for at least 1 hour.

In a bowl, combine the pork, bread, bacon, and the 3 tablespoons oil. Season with ¾ teaspoon salt and ¼ teaspoon pepper. Add the paprika and sage and toss gently but thoroughly. Let stand for 15 minutes. The bread should be well coated with the oil; if it isn't, toss again.

Thread the ingredients onto the skewers, alternating the pork, sage leaves, bread, and bacon, and putting a bacon square next to each bread cube. Wrap about 2 inches (5 cm) of the blunt end of each skewer with aluminum foil to make a handle.

Prepare a charcoal or gas grill for direct-heat grilling over medium-high heat, or preheat a cast-iron stove-top grill pan over medium-high heat. Lightly coat the grill rack or pan with oil. Place the skewers on the grill rack over the hottest part of the fire or in the grill pan, and cook until the pork is firm and lightly golden and the bread is golden brown and crisp, about 4 minutes per side. Move the skewers after 1 minute if the fire flares up.

Remove the foil from the skewers and arrange on plates. Serve at once with the lemon wedges.

## PORK TENDERLOIN, BREAD, AND BACON KEBABS WITH SAGE

 MAKES 4 SERVINGS

1 pork tenderloin, about 1 lb (500 g), silverskin removed and trimmed of excess fat

20 cubes coarse country bread, each about ¾ inch (2 cm)

3 slices bacon, cut into 16 squares, each about ¾ inch (2 cm)

3 tablespoons olive oil, plus extra for grill

Kosher salt and freshly ground pepper

½ teaspoon smoked paprika

20 large fresh sage leaves

Lemon wedges for serving

### A NOTE FROM THE BUTCHER

When removing silverskin, it is easier to insert your knife near the tapered end of the silverskin and to cut toward the thick end. Keep the knife edge tilted up against the silverskin slightly, and the knife will glide between the skin and the meat. If you cut the other direction, you are fighting the grain and the knife can dig into the loin, causing choppy cuts.

—Mark Martin, Nelson's Meat Market, Cedar Rapids, IA

# GRILLED DOUBLE-CUT PORK CHOPS WITH RHUBARB MOSTARDA

 MAKES 4 SERVINGS

Pork marries well with many fruits, and in the spring, I like to serve it with this rhubarb-mustard condiment, known as *mostarda* in Italy. I recommend making the *mostarda* the day before, which will allow its complex flavors to meld. Purchase chops from the rib end for the most flavor. If you are cooking over charcoal, be sure to create a cooler area on the grill where you can finish cooking these big, thick chops.

**FOR THE RHUBARB MOSTARDA**

⅔ cup (5 oz/155 g) sugar

⅓ cup (3 fl oz/80 ml) red wine vinegar

1 tablespoon peeled and minced fresh ginger

2 cloves garlic, minced

1 teaspoon ground cumin

1½ lb (750 g) rhubarb, trimmed and cut into ½-inch (12-mm) chunks

½ small red onion, finely chopped

2 tablespoons dry mustard

Freshly ground pepper

3 tablespoons fresh lemon juice

2 tablespoons olive oil

2 small cloves garlic, minced

Kosher salt and freshly ground pepper

4 double-cut pork chops, each about 1 lb (500 g) and 1½ inches (4 cm) thick

2 tablespoons coarsely chopped fresh flat-leaf parsley (optional)

---

**A NOTE FROM THE BUTCHER**

For the most flavor in this dish, seek out pork breeds such as Duroc and Berkshire.

—Bryan Flannery, Bryan's Fine Foods, San Francisco, CA

---

To make the *mostarda*, in a large, heavy pot, combine the sugar, vinegar, ginger, garlic, and cumin. Place over low heat and bring to a simmer, stirring frequently to dissolve the sugar. Add the rhubarb and onion, raise the heat to medium-high, and cook, stirring frequently to break up the rhubarb, until the mixture thickens slightly, about 5 minutes. Stir in the mustard, season with pepper, and stir until smooth. Let cool completely. If desired, refrigerate overnight. Return to room temperature before serving.

In a shallow nonreactive dish that will hold the chops in one layer, whisk together the lemon juice, oil, and garlic. Whisk in ½ teaspoon salt and season with pepper. Place the chops in the dish and brush both sides thoroughly with the lemon mixture. Cover and refrigerate for at least 1 hour or up to 3 hours, turning the chops occasionally.

Remove the chops from the refrigerator and let stand at room temperature for 20 minutes. Lift the chops from the marinade and pat dry. Reserve the marinade if using a charcoal grill.

Prepare a charcoal or gas grill for direct-heat grilling over medium-high heat, or preheat a cast-iron stove-top grill pan over medium-high heat. Place the chops on the grill rack over the hottest part of the fire or in the grill pan, and cook without moving them for 2½–3 minutes. Move the chops after 1 minute if the fire flares up. Turn and cook until the chops are golden brown and crusty, 2½–3 minutes more. If using a charcoal grill, brush the chops occasionally with the reserved marinade. Move the chops to a cooler part of the grill or reduce the heat, and continue to cook until the chops are firm to the touch but still have a little give, 10–12 minutes. Transfer to a platter, tent loosely with aluminum foil, and let rest for 3–4 minutes.

Garnish with the parsley, if desired, and serve at once with the *mostarda*.

Jerk seasoning, a combination of chiles and other spices that has come to be used around the world, originated in Jamaica. Here, it lends a fiery kick to a cut of pork—the tenderloin—that because of its leanness requires a powerful flavoring component. The habanero is one of the hottest chiles, so you can decide how many you are brave enough to include. The plum relish, with its refreshing lime juice and mint, helps tame the heat.

## JERK-SPICED PORK KEBABS WITH PLUM RELISH

 MAKES 4 SERVINGS

In a food processor, combine the white and green onions, chiles, allspice, thyme, nutmeg, oil, ¾ teaspoon salt, and ¼ teaspoon pepper. Process until puréed, then scoop out into a baking dish. Add the pork cubes, and toss to coat evenly. Cover and refrigerate for at least 1 hour or up to 4 hours. If using bamboo skewers, soak 8 skewers in water for at least 1 hour.

To make the relish, in a nonreactive bowl, stir together the plums, bell pepper (if using), onion, hot sauce, lime juice, mint, and cilantro. Set aside.

Remove the pork from the refrigerator and let stand at room temperature for 20–30 minutes. Prepare a charcoal or gas grill for direct-heat grilling over medium-high heat, or preheat a cast-iron stove-top grill pan over medium-high heat. Thread the pork cubes onto the skewers, pressing them snugly together. Wrap about 2 inches (5 cm) of the blunt end of each skewer in aluminum foil to make a handle. Pat the pork dry.

Place the skewers on the grill rack over the hottest part of the fire or in the grill pan, and cook until the pork is seared on all sides, browned, and firm, about 1½ minutes per side.

Remove the foil from the skewers and arrange on plates. Top with the relish and serve at once.

1 white or yellow onion, thickly sliced

4 green onions, white and green parts, thickly sliced

2 or 3 habanero chiles, seeded

2 teaspoons ground allspice

2 teaspoons dried thyme

1 teaspoon ground nutmeg

2 tablespoons canola oil

Kosher salt and freshly ground pepper

1 pork tenderloin, about 1¼ lb (625 g), silverskin removed, cut into ¾-inch (2-cm) cubes

### FOR THE PLUM RELISH

3 plums, pitted and cut into ¼-inch (6-mm) dice

3 tablespoons finely diced red bell pepper (optional)

1½ tablespoons minced red onion

1–3 teaspoons hot sauce, such as Pickapeppa Jamaican

2 teaspoons fresh lime juice

8–12 fresh mint leaves, coarsely chopped

1½ teaspoons minced fresh cilantro

# GRILLED PORK CHOPS WITH CARAMELIZED PEACHES AND BASIL

MAKES 4 SERVINGS

This is the quintessential dish for warm nights when you feel like grilling outside. Sirloin chops are a little tougher than loin or rib chops, but they have an intense pork flavor. I pair the chops with two summer staples: sweet, ripe peaches and peppery fresh basil. Tossing the peaches in a touch of maple syrup before grilling helps caramelize them, and a drizzle of balsamic adds a welcome acidic bite.

4 bone-in pork loin or end-loin chops, each about 9 oz (280 g) and ¾ inch (2 cm) thick, trimmed of excess fat

2 teaspoons olive oil, plus extra for brushing

Kosher salt and freshly ground pepper

2 peaches, quartered and pitted

2 tablespoons maple syrup

2–3 teaspoons good-quality balsamic vinegar

Small fresh basil leaves for garnish

Remove the chops from the refrigerator and let stand for 30 minutes.

Brush the chops very lightly with oil and season both sides generously with salt and pepper. In a bowl, combine the peach quarters, maple syrup, and 2 teaspoons oil. Season with pepper. Toss to coat evenly. Set aside.

Prepare a charcoal or gas grill for direct-heat grilling over medium-high heat, or preheat a cast-iron stove-top grill pan over medium-high heat.

Place the chops on the grill rack over the hottest part of the fire or in the grill pan, and cook until golden, about 2 minutes. Move to a cooler part of the grill or reduce the heat and cook until the pork is firm and cooked through but not dry, 3–4 minutes more per side. Place the peaches over direct heat and sear, turning with tongs, until the cut sides are golden, 30–60 seconds total.

Transfer the chops and peaches to a platter and drizzle sparingly with the vinegar. Garnish with the basil and serve at once.

These burgers, made with ground pork shoulder, chorizo, and bacon, pack a lot of flavor. Letting the mixture rest in the refrigerator allows the seasonings to marry and develop. If fresh chorizo is unavailable, use a link of fresh, hot Italian sausage, increase the garlic to 4 cloves, and double the quantity of smoked paprika. For a more dressed up presentation, omit the rolls and serve the patties alongside Herbed Couscous (page 214).

# GRILLED THREE-PORK BURGERS

**MAKES 6 SERVINGS**

Place the pork on a baking sheet and freeze, uncovered, for 20 minutes.

In a food processor, combine the fennel, shallot, and garlic. Pulse until finely chopped and transfer to a large bowl. Add one-third of the chilled pork to the processor and pulse about 12 times until coarsely chopped; don't let it turn to mush. You may have to redistribute the pork to achieve an even texture. Scrape out into the bowl without compacting the meat. Repeat to chop the remaining cubes.

Using a fork, thoroughly mix in the chorizo, bacon, cumin, paprika, thyme, parsley, ¾ teaspoon salt, and ½ teaspoon pepper. Form 6 loosely packed patties, then gently flatten them to about 1 inch (2.5 cm) thick and 3½ inches (9 cm) in diameter. Refrigerate for at least 15 minutes or up to 6 hours. Cover with plastic wrap if chilling more than 1 hour.

Prepare a charcoal or gas grill for direct-heat grilling over medium-high heat, or preheat a cast-iron stove-top grill pan over medium-high heat. Season the burgers with salt and pepper. Place on the grill rack over the hottest part of the fire or in the grill pan, and cook, turning once, until an instant-read thermometer inserted into the center of a burger registers 155°–160°F (68°–71°C), 8–10 minutes total. Turn the burgers again if necessary. The center of each burger will be just barely pink.

Spread the bottoms of the rolls with mayonnaise. Add the lettuce, burgers, tomato slices, and tops of the rolls. Serve at once.

2 lb (1 kg) nicely marbled boneless pork shoulder, cut into 1-inch (2.5-cm) cubes

½ small fennel bulb, trimmed, cored, and cut into large chunks

1 shallot, quartered

3 cloves garlic

¼ lb (125 g) fresh, soft chorizo sausage, casing removed

3 oz (90 g) bacon, very finely chopped

2 teaspoons ground cumin

½ teaspoon smoked paprika

½ teaspoon dried thyme

1 tablespoon minced fresh flat-leaf parsley

Kosher salt and freshly ground pepper

6 crusty rolls, split and lightly toasted

Mayonnaise

6–12 crisp lettuce leaves

6 tomato slices

---

**A NOTE FROM THE BUTCHER**

If you are having a hard time finding the perfect chorizo for this recipe, andouille is a good substitution. When grinding pork at home, coarsely grind the well-chilled meat just once to preserve its texture.

—Amelia Posada, Lindy and Grundy's Meats, Los Angeles, CA

---

## BEYOND PORK & BEEF

Once you have mastered the technique of grinding pork and beef, you can apply the same rule to other meats, such as lamb, venison, and veal, as well as chicken and turkey. Choose fattier cuts, such as lamb shoulder. If the cut is lean—veal is the leanest of all—incorporate additional fat from the same animal or fatback (pork) until the mixture is about 20 percent fat by weight. Here are some flavoring suggestions:

**Lamb**  rosemary, pine nuts, oregano

**Venison**  juniper berries, dried cherries, ancho chile powder

**Veal**  lemon zest, tarragon, paprika

**Chicken**  chives, tarragon, dried apples, walnuts

**Turkey**  dried cranberries, sage, chestnuts

## USES FOR GROUND MEAT

Home-ground meat can be formed into superior burgers, meat loaf, or meatballs, or shaped around skewers. It can be stuffed inside grape leaves and hollowed-out vegetables, layered in a lasagna, added to a tomato-based ragù, or used in an enchilada or taco recipe.

You can grind meat and make sausage in your kitchen without having a devoted grinding machine or a supply of meat casings. The method here, perfect for the home cook, calls for coarsely grinding small batches of semifrozen meat cubes in a food processor. The mixture is then blended with seasonings to make free-form sausage that can be used right away in a wide range of recipes. Or it can be formed into shapes and frozen.

**CHOOSING THE MEAT**  Almost any cut of meat may be ground, but meat from the shoulder is the tastiest because of its supply of fat. If you select meat from any area other than the shoulder (for beef, this cut is known as "chuck"), you will need to compensate for the lower fat content. Otherwise, the resulting sausage mixture will be dry and won't hold together during cooking. Ideally, make sure your sausage is about 20 percent fat by weight. Pork shoulder and beef chuck are naturally composed of that much fat. For leaner cuts, like loin, add bacon, fatback, salt pork, or fat trimmed from a roast.

**PREPARING THE MEAT**  Cut the meat into 1-inch (2.5-cm) cubes and place on a baking sheet lined with parchment paper. The cubes should barely touch. Freeze until firm but not rock solid, about 25 minutes.

**GRINDING THE MEAT**  Working with about one-third of the meat cubes at a time, and leaving the remaining cubes in the freezer until needed, scatter the cubes evenly in the bowl of a food processor fitted with a very sharp metal blade. You want the blade to cut right through the fat without smearing it. Pulse, in 2-second bursts, about 12 times, until the meat is just coarsely chopped. You may have to remove the top of the processor and redistribute the meat to achieve an even chop. Transfer to a chilled bowl and grind the remaining meat.

**MIXING AND FORMING THE SAUSAGE**  Prepare the seasoning ingredients and add to the bowl holding the ground meat. Use a fork to blend the ingredients together thoroughly without compacting the meat. With clean hands, gently and quickly pick up the mixture and form shapes, if desired. Place on a plate and refrigerate for 1 hour to firm.

**COOKING THE SAUSAGE**  In a large nonstick or well-seasoned frying pan over low heat, warm 2 teaspoons canola oil. Add the sausages and cover the pan. Cook for 20 minutes, turning the sausages every 5 minutes or so. Uncover, raise the heat to medium-high, and cook the sausages, turning as necessary, just until they are evenly golden on all sides and an instant-read thermometer inserted into the center of a sausage registers 155°F (68°C). Transfer to a paper towel–lined plate to drain.

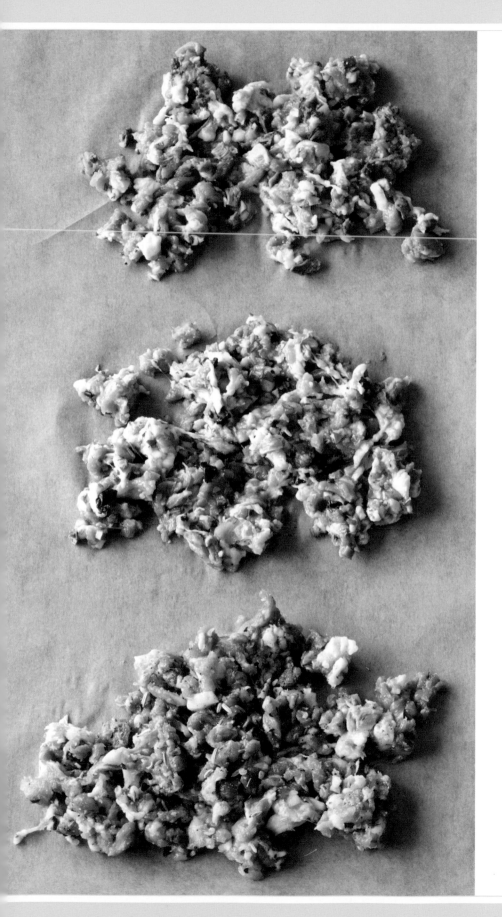

## BASIC SAUSAGE

MAKES 2 LB (1 KG)

2 lb (1 kg) boneless pork shoulder or pork butt

2 teaspoons fennel seeds

1–2 teaspoons ground coriander

1 tablespoon fine sea salt

2 teaspoons freshly ground black pepper

¼ teaspoon red pepper flakes

Grind the pork as directed at left and transfer to a chilled bowl. In a mini food processor, combine the fennel seeds, coriander, salt, black pepper, and pepper flakes. Process to a paste. Transfer the seasoning mixture to the bowl with the ground pork and mix with a fork. Use the sausage as is, or form into patties, torpedoes, or other shapes as directed in your recipe.

### CILANTRO-CHILE SEASONING

In a mini food processor, combine ½–1 jalapeño chiles, seeded and chopped; leaves from ½ bunch fresh cilantro, finely chopped; and 1 tablespoon each fine sea salt and freshly ground pepper. Add 2 tablespoons dark beer and the seasonings to the ground meat and mix.

### PORCINI-SAGE SEASONING

In a small bowl, soften ¾ oz (20 g) dried porcini mushrooms in hot water for 20 minutes. Drain, squeeze dry, and coarsely chop. In a food processor, combine the porcini; 2 shallots, sliced; 2 cloves garlic, sliced; leaves from 1 bunch fresh sage, sliced; 1 tablespoon fine sea salt; and 2 tablespoons freshly ground pepper. Add 2 tablespoons dry white wine and the seasonings to the ground meat and mix.

Many recipes instruct you to soak wood chips before grilling, but I have never found that this enhances the smoking process. The steam rising from the water in the drip pan keeps the meat from drying out during the long cooking. Serve the pork with Lime, Cabbage, and Jalapeño Slaw (page 214).

To make the spice rub, in a bowl, stir together the paprika, black pepper, sugar, kosher salt, celery salt, garlic powder, mustard, cumin, and cayenne.

Rinse the pork under cold running water. Pat dry thoroughly, including all the nooks and crannies. Rub the oil all over the pork, then rub in the spices, working them in well. Let stand at room temperature for 1½–2 hours.

Prepare a charcoal grill for indirect-heat grilling over medium heat, using hardwood charcoal, or prepare a gas grill for indirect grilling at about 300°F (150°C). Place a drip pan underneath the position on the grill rack where you will place the meat. Add about 2 cups (16 fl oz/500 ml) hot water to the drip pan, and if there is room, place a small pan of hot water on the grill rack. Be sure to leave room to add more coals as you cook.

Scatter a handful of oak, hickory, or fruit-wood chips over the hot coals, or, if using a gas grill, add the chips in a smoker box or foil packet, and place the pork on the grill rack over the drip pan. If you have a probe thermometer, insert it through the grill vents and into the center of the meat, without touching the bone. Cover the grill and maintain the temperature at 250°–300°F (120°–150°C). Cook the pork for 2½–5 hours. The timing will depend on the diameter of the meat, the ambient temperature, how many times you check the temperature, and whether you add hot or cold charcoal to replenish the spent coals. You will need to replenish the coals about once every hour, when the temperature starts to drop. Add 1 handful of wood chips the second time you add more charcoal or after about 2 hours in a gas grill. Don't worry if the temperature spikes higher, especially right after adding fresh charcoal.

The pork is done when it is fork-tender and the internal temperature registers 160°–165°F (71°–74°C). If you don't have a probe thermometer, use an instant-read thermometer. Don't check too often, however; every time you lift the lid, the heat loss slows down the cooking time.

Transfer the pork to a platter, tent loosely with aluminum foil, and let rest for 20 minutes. Carve into thick slices and serve at once.

# GRILL-SMOKED PORK SHOULDER WITH SPICE RUB

 SERVES 8

**FOR THE SPICE RUB**

⅓ cup (1 oz/30 g) sweet paprika

2 tablespoons freshly ground black pepper

2 tablespoons firmly packed dark brown sugar

1½ tablespoons kosher salt

2 teaspoons celery salt

2 teaspoons garlic powder

2 teaspoons dry mustard

2 teaspoons ground cumin

¾ teaspoon cayenne pepper

4½–6 lb (2.25–3 kg) bone-in pork shoulder, fat trimmed to about ⅛ inch (3 mm)

2 tablespoons canola oil

---

### A NOTE FROM THE BUTCHER

My favorite cut is pork shoulder. It is versatile and practically indestructible. Don't be afraid to leave on a little fat. The fat will render off during cooking, seasoning the meat at the same time.

—Otto Demke, Gepperth's Meat Market, Chicago, IL

---

## GRILLED BABY BACK RIBS WITH CITRUS BARBECUE SAUCE

 MAKES 6 SERVINGS

Baby back ribs are leaner and offer less meat by weight than spareribs. Their flavor is not quite as intense, so this preparation compensates with a long marinating time and a tangy sauce with a kick of spice. If you've never made your own barbecue sauce, this will be a revelation: citrus juices and honey add a depth and freshness lacking in bottled sauces.

¼ cup (¾ oz/20 g) sweet paprika

2 tablespoons Old Bay Seasoning

2 tablespoons chile powder

1–2 teaspoons cayenne pepper

2 teaspoons garlic powder

Kosher salt and freshly ground black pepper

1 tablespoon sugar

½ cup (4 fl oz/125 ml) balsamic vinegar

6 lb (3 kg) baby back ribs

### FOR THE BARBECUE SAUCE

1 small  yellow onion, sliced

1 cup (8 fl oz/250 ml) fresh orange juice

2 cups (1 lb/500 g) tomato ketchup

¼ cup (2 fl oz/60 ml) fresh lime juice

¼ cup (2 fl oz/60 ml) cider vinegar

2 tablespoons firmly packed dark brown sugar

1 tablespoon dry mustard

1 tablespoon sweet paprika

1½ teaspoons red pepper flakes

½ teaspoon garlic powder

½ teaspoon chile powder

1½–2 teaspoons hot-pepper sauce, such as Tabasco

1 tablespoon honey

Kosher salt and freshly ground black pepper

6 tablespoons (3 oz/90 g) unsalted butter

Sift the paprika, Old Bay, chile powder, cayenne, and garlic powder into a large bowl. Add 1 tablespoon each salt and pepper and the sugar. Add the vinegar and stir with a fork to make a paste. Rub the paste into the meat and wrap in plastic wrap. Place in a large roasting pan. Refrigerate overnight.

To prepare the barbecue sauce, in a blender or food processor, purée the onion with ¼ cup (2 fl oz/60 ml) of the orange juice until smooth, about 1 minute. Place the remaining ¾ cup (6 fl oz/180 ml) orange juice in a saucepan and add the ketchup, lime juice, vinegar, sugar, dry mustard, paprika, pepper flakes, garlic powder, chile powder, hot-pepper sauce, honey, 1 teaspoon salt, 1½ teaspoons black pepper, and butter. Stir in the onion purée. Bring to a slow simmer over low heat and cook, stirring occasionally, until thickened, about 25 minutes. Let cool.

Preheat the oven to 250°F (120°C). Line a rimmed baking sheet with aluminum foil. Place the ribs on the sheet. Cook, turning every hour, until the meat starts to pull away from the bones, about 3 hours. Remove the ribs from the oven and let rest for at least 10 minutes or up to 1 hour.

Prepare a charcoal or gas grill for direct-heat grilling over high heat. Place the ribs, meaty side down, on the grill rack and cook just until the fat starts to sizzle, 2–3 minutes. Turn and cook for 2–3 minutes more. Transfer to a cutting board. Cut between the ribs to separate them.

Mound the ribs on a platter and drizzle with the barbecue sauce, or pass the sauce at the table. Serve at once.

---

 **A NOTE FROM THE BUTCHER**

Ask the butcher to remove the membrane from the back of the rib plate. To remove it yourself, loosen it at the tail end of the rack, grasp it with a folded paper towel, and peel it off in one piece.

—Benjamin Dyer, Laurelhust Market, Portland, OR

---

The loin, a relatively lean cut of pork, works beautifully in this clean-tasting stew that is chunky and hearty enough to satisfy die-hard chili fans. The ingredients are cut into bite-sized pieces so that the distinctive flavors of the vegetables—tomatillos, tomatoes, and carrots—shine through. When serving cheese aficionados, sprinkle each bowl with shredded pepper jack.

# PORK AND TOMATILLO STEW

**MAKES 4 SERVINGS**

Place a Dutch oven or other large, heavy pot over high heat and add the oil. Season the pork generously with salt and pepper. Add to the pot and sear on all sides until browned, about 2 minutes per side. Add the onion, reduce the heat to medium, and cook, stirring occasionally, until the onion is softened, about 7 minutes.

Add the chile, garlic, chile powder, cumin, oregano, and ½ teaspoon salt. Cook, stirring frequently, until the mixture is aromatic, about 3 minutes. Add the flour, stir to make a paste, and cook for 1 minute more. Whisk in the broth and bring to a simmer. Add the carrot, potatoes, tomatoes, and tomatillos. Cover partially and simmer over low heat until the pork is very tender, about 45 minutes.

With a slotted spoon, transfer the pork to a plate. Continue to simmer the stew over medium-high heat until thickened, about 10 minutes. Shred the pork with 2 forks. Return the pork to the stew and season with salt, pepper, and hot sauce.

Ladle the stew into bowls, garnish with cilantro, and serve at once with tortilla chips.

2 tablespoons canola oil

1 boneless pork loin, about 1½ lb (750 g), cut into 2-inch (5-cm) chunks

Kosher salt and freshly ground pepper

1 yellow onion, roughly chopped

1 jalapeño chile, seeded and finely diced

3 cloves garlic, minced

2 teaspoons mild chile powder

1 tablespoon ground cumin

Pinch of dried oregano

1 tablespoon all-purpose flour

1¾ cups (14 fl oz/430 ml) reduced-sodium chicken broth

1 carrot, peeled and cut into ½-inch (12-mm) dice

¾ lb (375 g) russet potatoes, peeled and cut into 1-inch (2.5-cm) dice

1 can (28 oz/875 g) diced tomatoes, thoroughly drained

1 lb (500 g) tomatillos, husked, rinsed, and cut into 1-inch (2.5-cm) dice

Hot-pepper sauce, such as Tabasco

Chopped fresh cilantro for garnish

Corn tortilla chips for serving

### A NOTE FROM THE BUTCHER

All pork is not the same. When selecting top-quality pork, look for firm texture and the same fine-grain marbling you find in prime beef. Make sure that the pork is cut from the shoulder end of the loin rather than the sirloin end, which tends to be drier and less tender. For an excellent alternative cut, try well-marbled, boneless, pure-bred Berkshire pork shoulder.

—Robert Fleming, Alexander's Prime Meats and Catering, San Gabriel, CA

## CUBAN-STYLE SLOW-ROASTED PORK SHOULDER WITH MOJO SAUCE

 MAKES 6 SERVINGS

This slightly unconventional method of slow-roasting pork shoulder could be called "no roasting" (see Residual-Heat Roasting on page 12). It yields a deeply caramelized, crispy crust and a tender, juicy interior. Be sure to trim away any large pockets of fat on the meat before applying the seasonings. The citrusy *mojo* sauce used here, a version of the classic Cuban staple, provides a delicious contrast to the rich meat.

1 boneless pork shoulder, about 3 lb (1.5 kg), trimmed of excess fat

Kosher salt and freshly ground pepper

½ teaspoon ground cumin

½ teaspoon garlic powder

2 tablespoons olive oil

### FOR THE MOJO SAUCE

1 small red onion, cut into ⅛-inch (3-mm) dice

Grated zest of 2 oranges

½ cup (4 fl oz/125 ml) fresh orange juice

¼ cup (2 fl oz/60 ml) fresh lime juice

6 cloves garlic, minced

¾ cup (1 oz/30 g) minced fresh flat-leaf parsley

Kosher salt and freshly ground pepper

¾ cup (6 fl oz/180 ml) extra-virgin olive oil

Remove the pork from the refrigerator and let stand at room temperature for 1 hour.

In a small bowl, stir together 1½ teaspoons salt, a generous grinding of pepper, the cumin, the garlic powder, and 1 tablespoon of the oil. Rub all over the pork, working it into any nooks and crannies.

Preheat the oven to 450°F (230°C).

Heat a large, heavy roasting pan over high heat until it is very hot, about 3 minutes. Add the remaining 1 tablespoon oil and place the pork, fattier side down, in the pan. Reduce the heat to medium-high and sear until deep golden brown, about 6 minutes. Turn and sear for 5 minutes more. Insert an ovenproof meat thermometer into the thickest part of the meat. Place the pan in the center of the oven so that the thermometer is visible through the window in the oven door. Roast for 15 minutes. Reduce the oven temperature to 325°F (165°C) and roast for 30 minutes more. Turn off the oven and let the pork rest in the oven for 1 hour, without opening the oven door. Monitor the temperature; it should reach 150°–155°F (65°–68°C).

Meanwhile, prepare the *mojo* sauce: In a nonreactive bowl, combine the onion, orange zest, orange juice, lime juice, garlic, and parsley. Add 1¼ teaspoons salt and ¾ teaspoon pepper. Stir to blend. (The sauce can be made up to 12 hours in advance, covered tightly, and refrigerated; return to room temperature before serving.)

Set the oven temperature to 450°F (230°C). Roast the pork for 15 minutes to warm the exterior; the internal temperature will not change. Remove from the oven and let rest, loosely covered with aluminum foil, for 10 minutes.

Cut across the grain into slices about ¼ inch (6 mm) thick. Arrange on a platter, top with the sauce, and serve at once.

Since ham has a very rich flavor and a lot of salt, I like to serve it with a sauce that offers bracing acidity—in the form of balsamic vinegar and cornichons—as a counterpoint. The easiest way to mince parsley is to process it in a mini food processor. The leaves should be rinsed and spun thoroughly dry, or they will clump together and resist chopping.

## BALSAMIC-GLAZED HAM WITH PARSLEY-CORNICHON GREMOLATA

 MAKES 10–12 SERVINGS

Remove the ham from the refrigerator and let stand at room temperature for 2 hours.

Preheat the oven to 250°F (120°C). Line a large, heavy roasting pan with aluminum foil. Trim the fat on the ham to ¼–½ inch (6–12 mm), if necessary, and score in a diamond pattern. Place the ham, cut side down, in the pan and cover tightly with foil. Bake for 10 minutes per pound (500 g).

In a small bowl, combine the vinegar, sugar, and mustard. Whisk into a thin paste.

Remove the foil from the ham and brush the mustard mixture generously all over the exposed surface of the ham. Raise the oven temperature to 425°F (220°C) and roast the ham, basting it every 5 minutes or so with the mustard mixture, until dark and glossy, 15–20 minutes. Let the ham rest for 20–45 minutes.

To make the *gremolata,* in a nonreactive bowl, whisk together the parsley, cornichons and brine, capers, green onions, olive oil, and vinegar. Whisk in ¼ teaspoon salt and ½ teaspoon pepper.

Cut the ham into slices and serve at once with the *gremolata.*

½ fully cooked bone-in ham, preferably from the shank end, 6½–8 lb (3.25–4 kg)

¼ cup (2 fl oz/60 ml) balsamic vinegar

1 cup (7 oz/220 g) firmly packed dark brown sugar

1½ tablespoons dry mustard

**FOR THE PARSLEY-CORNICHON GREMOLATA**

1 cup (1 oz/30 g) firmly packed fresh flat-leaf parsley, minced

10 cornichons, minced, plus 1 teaspoon brine

¼ cup (2 oz/60 g) capers, rinsed and coarsely chopped

3 green onions, white and light green parts, minced

½ cup (4 fl oz/125 ml) extra-virgin olive oil

2 tablespoons white wine vinegar

Kosher salt and freshly ground pepper

### A NOTE FROM THE BUTCHER

Most hams sold today are actually half hams, cut from a whole leg of pork. A butt-end ham comes from the upper thigh, and a shank-end ham comes from lower down the leg. A butt-end ham tends to be a little more expensive than a shank-end ham, and some say it has a meatier flavor, though it has more gristle and bone to work around. I am in the shank-is-better camp: I find that it yields lovely, juicy red meat and is easier to carve.

—Ron Savenor, Savenor's Market, Boston, MA

## MEATBALLS IN ROMESCO SAUCE

MAKES 4–6 SERVINGS

Meatballs are appreciated around the world, perhaps because they're so enjoyable to eat. I like to serve my meatballs in *romesco* sauce, a punchier Spanish version of a tomato sauce that is full of garlic, roasted peppers, and ground nuts. I like to serve the meatballs cold, but if you serve them hot, be sure to warm the sauce in a double boiler, or it may scorch. The meatballs and sauce store well in the refrigerator for up to 3 days.

### FOR THE ROMESCO SAUCE

4 slices coarse country bread, crusts removed and torn into chunks

6 tablespoons (3 fl oz/90 ml) red wine vinegar

⅔ cup (3 oz/90 g) slivered almonds

2 cloves garlic

½ cup (3½ oz/105 g) canned diced tomatoes with juice

2 canned roasted piquillo peppers, drained

2 teaspoons smoked paprika

Kosher salt

½ cup (4 fl oz/125 ml) extra-virgin olive oil

### FOR THE MEATBALLS

6 slices sandwich-style white bread, crusts removed

¾ cup (6 fl oz/180 ml) whole milk

½ lb (250 g) ground pork

¼ lb (125 g) ground beef chuck (20 percent fat)

1 small white or yellow onion, finely chopped

¼ cup (⅓ oz/10 g) minced fresh flat-leaf parsley and/or dill

1 tablespoon dried oregano

¼ cup (1 oz/30 g) grated Parmesan cheese

1 large egg, lightly beaten

Kosher salt and freshly ground pepper

To make the *romesco* sauce, place the bread chunks in a bowl, add the vinegar, toss to coat, and let soften for about 10 minutes. In a small, dry frying pan over medium heat, toast the almonds, stirring, until just golden, about 5 minutes. Transfer to a plate and let cool completely.

Drop the garlic cloves into a food processor with the motor running, and process until the pieces stop moving. Add the almonds and pulse until grainy. Add the bread and vinegar mixture, tomatoes, peppers, paprika, and ½ teaspoon salt and process until smooth. With the motor running, add the oil in a slow, steady stream and process just until emulsified or thoroughly mixed. Taste and adjust the seasoning. Cover and refrigerate for 1 hour to allow the flavors to marry. The sauce will keep in the refrigerator for up to 3 days.

To make the meatballs, in a small bowl, soak the bread in the milk for 10 minutes, turning to moisten it evenly. Squeeze most of the milk from the bread and tear it into small pieces. In a large bowl, combine the bread, pork, beef, onion, parsley, oregano, Parmesan, egg, ½ teaspoon salt, and a good grinding of pepper. Blend with a fork, breaking up the ground meat, and then, with clean hands, mix thoroughly. Chill for 1 hour.

Line a rimmed baking sheet with parchment paper. Use an ice-cream scoop to form about 18 meatballs the size of golf balls, placing them on the prepared sheet. Chill again for 1 hour.

Place the *romesco* sauce in the top of a double boiler over gently simmering water and cover. Preheat the broiler and place a rack about 3 inches (7.5 cm) from the heat source. Slide the baking sheet in the broiler and brown the meatballs, turning them once or twice with tongs, until golden brown and firm, 8–15 minutes. To test the meatballs, cut into one to make sure it is no longer pink at the center. Transfer the meatballs to the warm sauce. Cover and cook for 5 minutes, turning the meatballs occasionally and spooning the sauce over the top. Serve at once.

# PORK RIB RAGÚ WITH PENNE

MAKES 4–6 SERVINGS

I call this my Sunday ragù, because it's the perfect cool-weather dish for when you want to hunker down and spend a day at home. The hearty sauce can also be made with boneless St. Louis–style ribs, which will yield a leaner result for the chunky sauce (and require about 30 minutes less cooking time). But as usual, when bones are involved, as they are with the spareribs, the flavor will be richer and gloriously meaty.

1 tablespoon olive oil

¼ lb (125 g) pancetta, diced

3 lb (1.5 kg) pork spareribs, cut into individual ribs

Kosher salt and freshly ground pepper

1 white or yellow onion, finely chopped

3 ribs celery, finely chopped

6 cloves garlic, minced

1 bay leaf

3 fresh thyme sprigs

2 cups (16 fl oz/500 ml) dry red wine, such as Syrah

1 can (28 oz/875 g) chopped tomatoes, preferably San Marzano

1½ lb (750 g) penne pasta

1¼ cups (10 oz/315 g) whole-milk ricotta

⅔ cup (2½ oz/75 g) grated Parmesan cheese

Handful of coarsely chopped fresh herbs, such as flat-leaf parsley, basil, and/or dill

Place a large Dutch oven or other heavy pot over medium heat and add the oil and pancetta. Stir until the pancetta is lightly browned and renders some fat, about 10 minutes. With a slotted spoon, transfer to a platter. Season the ribs all over with salt and pepper. Add half of the ribs to the pot, raise the heat to medium-high, and cook, turning as necessary with tongs, until browned on all sides, 8–10 minutes. Transfer to the platter and brown the remaining ribs.

Preheat the oven to 325°F (165°C).

Add the onion and celery to the pot, cover, reduce the heat to medium, and cook, stirring occasionally, until softened, about 10 minutes. Stir in the garlic, bay leaf, and thyme and cook for 1 minute more. Add the wine and deglaze the pot thoroughly, stirring to scrape up the browned bits from the bottom. Bring to a simmer and cook until the liquid is reduced by about one-third. Return the pancetta and ribs to the pot, add the tomatoes and ½ teaspoon salt, and season with pepper. Cover, place in the oven, and cook, turning and distributing the ribs every once in a while, until the meat is falling off the bones, 2–2½ hours. If the liquid begins to evaporate, stir in 1 or 2 tablespoons water.

Let cool slightly, then remove the bones, shredding the meat as you go and returning it to the pot. The sauce should be quite thick. Let stand for a few minutes, then tip the pot and spoon off some of the fat from the edges. Repeat while you cook the pasta.

Bring a large pot of salted water to a boil and cook the penne until al dente, according to the package instructions. Drain well and place in a large bowl. Add the ricotta, about two-thirds of the sauce, the Parmesan, and the herbs. Toss to distribute the ingredients evenly, then top with the remaining sauce. Serve at once.

In Italy, a similarly seasoned roast, called porchetta, is made using a whole boned pig with the skin intact—the outcome is teeth-shatteringly crisp. Here's an easier, and smaller, version for the home cook. This amazingly juicy roast is just as delicious at room temperature—the way it is served at Italian street markets every weekend. That means you can cook it the day before a party. Leftovers are great in sandwiches.

## ROASTED HERB-STUFFED PORK LOIN

MAKES 8–10 SERVINGS

Begin preparing the pork 2 days before serving. The pork will have a pocket from which the bones were removed. Make a cut down the length of the pork loin, cutting from one side to the other without cutting all the way through and following the muscle of the meat. Open the pork roughly flat. It should resemble a large, lumpy rectangle. Now "butterfly" it a little by cutting 1 inch (2.5 cm) or so into the thickest parts of the meat, then opening them out, sort of like a book (see page 166). The rectangle should be about 1 inch (2.5 cm) thick. Place on a large rimmed platter.

Bruise the peppercorns, coriander, and bay leaves slightly in a mortar with a pestle, or pulse a few times in a mini food processor. Transfer to a bowl. Stir in ¾ teaspoon salt for each pound (500 g) of meat. Rub the spice mixture into both sides of the pork, concentrating it on the thicker parts. Cover and refrigerate the pork for 48 hours.

Remove the pork from the refrigerator and rinse briefly under cold running water to remove the spice mixture. Pat thoroughly dry. Let stand at room temperature for 1½ hours.

Preheat the oven to 450°F (230°C). In a mini food processor, pulse the garlic until finely chopped. Add the fennel seeds, rosemary, sage, lemon zest, and the 3 tablespoons oil. Add ½ teaspoon salt and season with pepper. Pulse to form a paste. Spread the paste over the inside of the pork, then roll the meat into a cylinder about 4 inches (10 cm) in diameter, and tie with a kitchen string at even intervals (see page 166). Make sure that the exterior of the pork is completely dry. Brush with oil and season generously with pepper. Place in a roasting pan.

Roast for 30 minutes. Reduce the oven temperature to 325°F (165°C) and roast until an instant-read thermometer inserted into the center of the roast registers 140°F (60°C), 20–25 minutes. Remove from the oven, tent loosely with aluminum foil, and let rest for 15–30 minutes.

Snip the strings and cut crosswise into thick slices. Serve at once.

1 boneless pork loin, 4½–6 lb (2.25–3 kg), trimmed of any excess fat

1 tablespoon peppercorns

1 tablespoon coriander seeds

4 bay leaves, crumbled

Kosher salt and freshly ground pepper

10 cloves garlic

2 tablespoons fennel seeds

1 tablespoon minced fresh rosemary

1 tablespoon minced fresh sage

Grated zest of 2 lemons

3 tablespoons olive oil, plus extra for brushing

 **A NOTE FROM THE BUTCHER**

Try leaving a layer of fat on one side of the roast to help keep this lean cut moist during cooking. You can always trim it off before serving.

—Frank Ottomanelli, O. Ottomanelli & Sons Prime Meat Market, New York, NY

Some of the classic elements of Asian cuisine are showcased in this chunky lemongrass-perfumed marinade. The final browning of the ribs is done in the broiler, but if yours cannot achieve high heat, you may want to finish the ribs in a 500°F (260°C) oven or on a hot grill. They will be cooked at that point—the goal is to create a crispy crust quickly.

## OVEN-BROWNED SPARERIBS WITH LEMONGRASS, HONEY, AND SOY

 MAKES 6–8 SERVINGS

In a large roasting pan or baking dish, whisk together the lemongrass, ginger, garlic, honey, soy sauce, fish sauce, oil, and lime juice. Whisk in ½ teaspoon salt and season with pepper. Poke the ribs with a small, sharp knife every 3–4 inches (7.5–10 cm), to allow the marinade to penetrate the meat. Place the ribs in the pan and turn to coat evenly, rubbing the marinade into the nooks and crannies. Cover and refrigerate for at least 6 hours or up to overnight, turning the ribs occasionally.

Remove the ribs from the refrigerator and let stand at room temperature for 30 minutes. Preheat the oven to 250°F (120°C) and position one rack in the middle and another rack in the lower third.

Line 2 rimmed baking sheets with aluminum foil and place a wire rack in each pan. Arrange the ribs on the racks, meaty side up, and spoon the remaining marinade over the tops. Bake without moving the ribs for 3½ hours, switching the positions of the pans halfway through.

Remove the ribs from the oven and let rest for at least 10 minutes or up to 1 hour. Discard the greasy foil lining the pans, replace with clean foil, and return the ribs to the racks in the pans, meaty side up.

Preheat the broiler and place an oven rack about 4 inches (10 cm) from the heat source. Broil each rack of ribs just until the fat starts to sizzle and crisp, 3–4 minutes. Turn and broil for 2–3 minutes more. Let cool for 5 minutes, then cut between the ribs to separate them. Squeeze the lime wedges over the ribs, garnish with the basil, and serve at once.

4 lemongrass stalks, pale inner parts only, finely chopped

⅓ cup (2 oz/60 g) pickled red ginger, minced

6 large cloves garlic, minced

⅓ cup (4 oz/125 g) honey

⅓ cup (3 fl oz/80 ml) reduced-sodium soy sauce

3 tablespoons Thai or Vietnamese fish sauce

3 tablespoons peanut oil

Juice of 1 large lime

Kosher salt and freshly ground pepper

2 racks pork spareribs, about 6 lb (3 kg) total weight

1 lime, quartered

¼ cup (⅓ oz/10 g) coarsely chopped fresh basil, preferably Thai

 **A NOTE FROM THE BUTCHER**

Ask the butcher to remove the membrane from the bone side of a rack of spareribs. It is very tough, even when cooked for a long time.

—Larry Jobin, The Meat Shop, Phoenix, AZ

# ROASTED PORK TENDERLOIN WITH FENNEL SEED AND BREAD CRUMB CRUST

**MAKES 4 SERVINGS**

These tenderloins are deliciously crusty and easily carved into medallions for a festive fall dinner. I like to serve them on a platter with sautéed rainbow chard and roasted sweet potato wedges. Care must be taken not to overcook the tenderloins. I cook the pork to 140°F (60°C) because it is perfectly safe and far juicier than if cooked to 170°F (77°C), the recommended doneness temperature in decades past.

2 pork tenderloins, 10–12 oz (315–375 g) each, silverskin removed and trimmed of excess fat

2 teaspoons white vinegar

1 tablespoon coarsely crushed fennel seeds

1 teaspoon coarsely ground pepper

½ teaspoon dried oregano

½ teaspoon dried thyme

Kosher salt

2 tablespoons olive oil

1 large shallot, finely chopped

1 clove garlic, minced

⅓ cup (1½ oz/45 g) fine dried bread crumbs

Rub each tenderloin with 1 teaspoon of the vinegar, then place in a shallow baking dish. In a small bowl, combine the fennel seeds, pepper, oregano, thyme, and 1 teaspoon salt. Rub each tenderloin all over with half of the seasoning mixture. Cover with plastic wrap and refrigerate for at least 4 hours or up to overnight.

Remove the tenderloins from the refrigerator and let stand at room temperature for 30 minutes. Preheat the oven to 400°F (200°C). Place a rack on a rimmed baking sheet.

In a small frying pan over low heat, warm the oil. Add the shallot and cook until softened but not brown, 4–5 minutes. Add the garlic and bread crumbs, raise the heat to medium-high, and cook, stirring, until the crumbs are toasted and fragrant, about 3 minutes. Let cool.

Transfer the crumb mixture to a plate and break up any clumps with a fork. Spread in an even layer. Roll each tenderloin in the bread crumb mixture, pressing to help the mixture adhere firmly all around.

Carefully transfer the tenderloins to the baking sheet. Roast until the crust is crisp and brown and an instant-read thermometer inserted into a tenderloin at the thickest point registers 140°F (60°C), about 25 minutes. Remove from the oven and let rest for 5 minutes. Cut crosswise into thick slices and serve at once.

---

**A NOTE FROM THE BUTCHER**

Pork tenderloin can be compared to filet mignon—it is the most tender of all pork cuts. It is much leaner than beef, however. For example, 3 ounces (90 g) of pork tenderloin have 120 calories and 3 grams fat, but the same amount of beef tenderloin has 175 calories and 8.1 grams fat.

—Phil Lucas, The Meat Shop, Phoenix, AZ

---

For an authentic Italian experience, accompany this unctuous roast with *farro*, a rustic, barleylike wheat. You could trim all the excess fat from the roast before braising, but leaving on about ¼ inch (6 mm) of fat here and there will contribute to the meat's juiciness. At serving time, scoop up the curdlike sauce with a slotted spoon, leaving the fat behind.

Remove the pork shoulder from the refrigerator and let stand at room temperature for 1–1½ hours.

Preheat the oven to 325°F (165°C).

Season the roast generously all over with salt and pepper. In a Dutch oven or other large, ovenproof pot over medium-high heat, melt 1 tablespoon of the butter with the oil. Add the pork, fat side down, and sear for 3–4 minutes. Repeat to brown all sides, about 15 minutes total. Adjust the heat level so that the meat sizzles actively but does not scorch. Transfer the pork to a platter and pour off the fat from the pot.

Return the pot to medium heat and melt the remaining 2 tablespoons butter. Add the sage leaves. Cook for 1 minute. Stirring constantly, slowly pour in the milk and cream. Return the pork to the pot, fat side up, and add the bay leaves, lemon zest, and 1 teaspoon salt. Season generously with pepper. When the liquid begins to steam, partially cover the pot and transfer to the oven.

Cook the pork, turning it every 30 minutes, for 2 hours. Uncover and continue to cook until very tender, 30–60 more, again turning after 30 minutes if cooking for longer than 30 minutes more. Transfer the pork to a platter and let the pan sauce settle.

With a slotted spoon, remove the curds from the sauce, leaving behind the fat, and transfer to a fine-mesh sieve set over a small saucepan. Push the curds through the sieve to make a smooth, creamy sauce. Warm the sauce over low heat and stir in the lemon juice. Taste and adjust the seasoning. The sauce should be subtly tart from the lemon and slightly peppery, to cut the pork's richness. Cut the pork into thick chunks and serve at once, passing the sauce at the table.

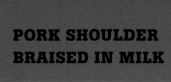

## PORK SHOULDER BRAISED IN MILK

 MAKES 6–8 SERVINGS

1 boneless pork shoulder, 3½–4 lb (1.75–2 kg), trimmed of excess fat

Kosher salt and freshly ground pepper

3 tablespoons unsalted butter

1 tablespoon olive oil

25 fresh sage leaves, coarsely chopped

4 cups (32 fl oz/1 l) whole milk

1 cup (8 fl oz/250 ml) heavy cream

3 bay leaves

Zest from 1 lemon, removed in wide strips with a vegetable peeler

1 teaspoon fresh lemon juice

### A NOTE FROM THE BUTCHER

One of Marczyk's favorite cuts! Pork shoulder has more fat and connective tissue than a roast or chop, but it is also packed with flavor. When braising shoulder, make sure you cook it until it is "falling apart" tender. For the fullest flavor, sear it first to brown the exterior well. Then "set it and forget it!"

—James Cross, Marczyk Fine Foods, Denver, CO

# ROASTED RACK OF PORK WITH FENNEL SEED, LAVENDER, AND GARLIC PASTE

 **MAKES 6 SERVINGS**

This dish is inspired by the flavors of the Mediterranean: fennel is a classic partner for pork in Italy, and the touch of lavender evokes the French countryside. You can ask the butcher to french the bones, but I also like to leave them rustic and whole. I don't want to be deprived of the crispy meat between the bones.

1½ teaspoons fennel seeds

1 teaspoon dried thyme

1 teaspoon dried lavender

Kosher salt and freshly ground pepper

4 cloves garlic, minced

2 tablespoons olive oil

1 rack of pork, about 6½ lb (3.25 kg) and 6 ribs

2 tablespoons capers, rinsed

Grated zest of 2 lemons

In a mini food processor, combine the fennel seeds, thyme, and lavender. Pulse to blend and break up the seeds. Transfer to a small bowl and stir in 2 teaspoons salt, ¼ teaspoon pepper, the garlic, and 1 tablespoon of the oil to form a paste. Rub the paste into both sides and ends of the pork, concentrating the paste on the thicker, meaty side of the rack and using less on the cut ends. Place in a baking dish, cover loosely, and refrigerate for at least 24 hours or preferably 48 hours.

Remove the pork from the refrigerator and let stand at room temperature for about 30 minutes. Preheat the oven to 250°F (120°C). Line a rimmed baking sheet with aluminum foil.

In the food processor, combine the capers, lemon zest, and the remaining 1 tablespoon oil. Pulse until the capers and zest are finely ground, scraping down the bowl once or twice.

Place the rack, bone side down, on the baking sheet. Rub the caper-lemon mixture over the meaty side of the rack. Transfer the pan to the oven so that the bones face toward the back of the oven. Roast until an instant-read thermometer inserted into the pork at the thickest point registers 125°F (52°C), 1½–1¾ hours. Raise the oven temperature to 425°F (220°C) and continue to roast until the internal temperature reaches 140°F (60°C), about 20 minutes more. Transfer the rack to a cutting board, tent loosely with aluminum foil, and let rest for 10–15 minutes.

Cut between the bones into chops and serve at once.

---

**✄ A NOTE FROM THE BUTCHER**

A rack of pork is your best bet to avoid the "dry pork" syndrome. Much like a beef rib roast, it is naturally marbled, which keeps it moist. To keep it juicy, have your butcher cut through the chine bone between each rib rather than removing the entire chine. After letting the meat rest, grab the largest butcher knife you have and cut between the bones at the table to serve the chops with flair. Remember to watch the internal temperature like a hawk!

—Don Kuzaro, Jr., Don & Joe's Meats, Seattle, WA

---

# ROASTED FIVE-SPICE PORK SHOULDER WITH GREEN ONION SALSA

 MAKES 4–6 SERVINGS

Chinese cuisine embraces and celebrates pork shoulder—and for good reason. This richly marbled cut stands up beautifully to the dry-heat method of roasting. An added benefit is the crispy skin, which is enhanced with the baking soda technique used here. If you purchase a shoulder without its skin, trim the fat to ¼ inch (6 mm) and skip the 36-hour drying process.

1 skin-on, bone-in pork shoulder, 5½–6 lb (2.75–3 kg)

1½ teaspoons baking soda

Kosher salt and freshly ground pepper

2 teaspoons five-spice powder

3 cloves garlic, minced

### FOR THE GREEN ONION SALSA

4 green onions, white and light green parts, minced

2 teaspoons minced fresh cilantro

4 teaspoons rice vinegar

4 teaspoons medium-dry sherry

4 teaspoons Thai or Vietnamese fish sauce

2 teaspoons reduced-sodium soy sauce

1 teaspoon Asian sesame oil

1 teaspoon fresh lemon juice

---

**A NOTE FROM THE BUTCHER**

Don't let your butcher cut off too much of the fat from a pork shoulder. Guests expecting the more common loin roast may be surprised by the texture, but will also thrill at the rich taste.

—James Cross, Marczyk Fine Foods, Denver, CO

---

With a stiff wire brush (a clean grill brush works well), vigorously scrub the skin on the pork shoulder to create an uneven, textured surface. With an ice pick or meat thermometer, make lots of little pinpricks all over the skin (this takes muscle, so jab down hard). In a small bowl, combine the baking soda and 1½ teaspoons salt with 1 cup (8 fl oz/250 ml) water and stir to dissolve. Brush all over the skin side only. Place the pork, skin side up, on a rack set over a baking sheet and refrigerate, uncovered, for 36 hours.

Remove the pork from the refrigerator and let stand for 1–1½ hours. Preheat the oven to 425°F (220°).

With a sharp knife, score the meat side of the shoulder, making a crisscross pattern only ¼ inch (6 mm) deep. Work 1 teaspoon of the five-spice powder and two-thirds of the garlic into the meat. Turn the shoulder skin side up. With a heavy, sharp knife, make parallel cuts through the skin, but not into the meat, spacing them about 1 inch (2.5 cm) apart. Place the pork, skin side up, on a rack set over a roasting pan.

Place in the oven and roast for 45 minutes. In a small bowl, stir together the remaining 1 teaspoon five-spice powder, the remaining garlic, 2 teaspoons salt, and 1 teaspoon pepper. Scatter this mixture over the pork, concentrating it between the golden strips of skin. Reduce the oven temperature to 350°F (180°C) and continue to roast until the skin is blistered and golden and an instant-read thermometer inserted into the center of the meat, away from the bone, registers about 160°F (71°C), about 45 minutes longer. Let stand for about 30 minutes.

To prepare the salsa, in a bowl, stir together the green onions, cilantro, vinegar, sherry, fish sauce, soy sauce, sesame oil, and lemon juice.

Cut the shoulder between the strips of skin, releasing the meat from the bone so that each slice gets a strip of crispy skin. Arrange on a platter, top with spoonfuls of the salsa, and serve at once.

# LAMB

# LAMB PRIMER

Meat from lamb, or young sheep, is tender and distinctive in flavor. Major producers are found in the United States, New Zealand, Australia, England, and the Mediterranean region. More than any other meat you will find in the market, lamb can vary in its characteristics due to the diversity of the breeds and their diets and the climates where the animals were raised.

## GRADING AND AGE

The U.S. Department of Agriculture inspects all lamb but grades the meat only when requested. Of the five grades, prime is the highest, reflecting the high amount of marbling. Prime is mostly reserved for sale to restaurants, but you can seek it out at high-end retailers and farmers' markets. Choice is the only other grade you will find when you shop for lamb. Though the marbling is not as extensive as in prime cuts, choice lamb is still high quality.

Lamb is generally defined as meat from animals that are less than 1 year old. Most animals are brought to market at between 5 and 8 months of age. Occasionally you will find meat labeled "baby lamb," which means that the animal was less than 10 weeks old and weighed less than 20 pounds (10 kg) at the time of slaughter. "Spring lamb" refers to an animal weighing 20 to 40 pounds (10 to 20 kg) that was slaughtered between March and October. The tenderness of lamb is determined more by the age of the animal than by the extent of the marbling. The meat from young lamb is pale pink, very tender, and mild. As the lamb ages, the meat gains character and flavor, and darkens slightly in color.

## GRAIN FED VS GRASS FED

Most lamb sold in supermarkets, especially in the United States, comes from animals that have been fed grain and raised in feedlots. In the opinion of some food experts as well as consumers, meat from grass-fed lamb has a superior taste and a particularly tender texture. For these reasons, grass-fed lamb has gained converts and is increasingly available at butcher shops and specialty-food stores. You can do your own taste test comparing grain-fed and grass-fed lamb, and decide which type you prefer.

## LAMB FROM AROUND THE WORLD

Several qualities distinguish lamb raised in the United States from that raised in Australia and New Zealand. American cuts, especially from grain-fed animals, tend to be larger and carry more fat. In Australia and New Zealand, the animals feed on grass or other forage. The cuts are smaller and their meat has a fuller flavor than meat from animals fed exclusively on grain. Some consumers, depending on where they live, may be able to find only frozen lamb from Australia or New Zealand.

## LAMB AT A GLANCE

**Look for** slightly moist meat, light red color, white external fat, fine grain, smooth bones.

**Avoid** wet or sticky meat, deep red meat, blood spots, yellow fat, dry and porous-looking bones.

**Cuts to remember** neck, tenderloin.

**Best value** shoulder.

**Splurge cuts** rack of lamb, frenched rib chops.

**Storage** 3 to 5 days in the refrigerator; up to 6 months in the freezer.

## BEST FLAVORS FOR LAMB

**American flavors** garlic, mustard, thyme, dried fruit.

**Mediterranean flavors** rosemary, oregano, garlic, figs, prosciutto, anchovies, balsamic vinegar, lemon, sherry, tomatoes, olives.

**Middle Eastern flavors** yogurt, mint, dill, cumin, saffron, preserved lemon.

**Indian flavors** curry powder, onions, coconut milk.

The taste of grass-fed lamb is influenced by the type of forage. The well-known lamb from Brittany in France, for instance, grazes in the local salt marshes. As a result, the meat has a prized, subtly salty flavor.

## LAMB BASICS

**TRIMMING**  For most meats, leaving a margin of fat on the surface helps retain moisture and juiciness during cooking. For lamb, however, it is best to trim the fat more aggressively to avoid an overly gamy flavor. The thick membrane covering the meat, called the fell, will already have been trimmed away from smaller cuts by the butcher (it is sometimes left intact on larger cuts to help them retain their shape and juices as they cook), but you may still need to remove any excess pieces of fat.

**BRINGING TO ROOM TEMPERATURE**  All the lamb recipes in this book call for cooking meat that has been brought to room temperature. A lamb chop might need to stand only 10 minutes, whereas a leg of lamb might require up to 2 hours. For large cuts, you can use a probe thermometer to test the temperature at the center of the meat. When the temperature reaches about 55°F (13°C), the lamb is ready to cook. Meat that is cooked while still cold from the refrigerator will take longer to reach the proper doneness temperature.

**SEASONING**  Depending on the cut and the preparation, seasonings range from simple, such as fresh herbs, to assertive, such as curry. When searing, panfrying, or grilling chops or steaks, a generous sprinkling of salt and pepper is all that is needed. Various cuts can be cooked with stuffings combining fruit and nuts, olives and citrus, or sausage and leeks. Braising less tender cuts such as shoulder and shanks seasons the meat in a cooking liquid with flavors like citrus juice and herb sprigs or anchovies and shallot.

**RESTING**  Lamb, like other meat, benefits from resting after it is cooked, which allows the juices to settle and redistribute. The resting period varies from 3 to 5 minutes for a lamb chop to 30 minutes for a larger roast.

**STORING**  If you buy lamb in an airtight package from the supermarket, you should consume it within 2 days. Some stores sell vacuum-sealed lamb cuts; consult the printed directions on the packaging for length of storage. Well-marbled cuts like shoulder take better to freezing than leaner cuts like leg, loin, and tenderloin. For any cut that you want to freeze, enclose the lamb first in plastic wrap, then tightly in aluminum foil, seal securely, and freeze for up to 6 months. The safest method for thawing lamb is to let it stand in the refrigerator. Large roasts might need 2 days or more to thaw; smaller cuts such as chops will be ready in 1 day. Do not be tempted to thaw the frozen meat in a microwave or in hot water. Although the exterior will thaw, the center will remain frozen.

### FAQS FOR THE BUTCHER

**Q: I've always heard that younger lamb is best. Is that true?**

A: Many people talk adoringly of spring lamb, but I prefer older yearlings or hoggets, which aren't really considered lamb because of their age. Yearlings produce wider loin chops, which have thicker fat and darker red meat.

**Q: I like lamb chops, but they can be pricey. Is there a less expensive alternative?**

A: Try chops cut from the shoulder. They have more marbling than rib or loin chops, so they will be juicier and more flavorful.

**Q: What are some good "butcher's cuts" of lamb?**

A: I really like lamb belly. Like pork belly, it is rich and fatty, and perfect for rolling up and slow roasting.

**Q: I've purchased lamb from different butchers and grocery stores, and it all tastes different. Why?**

A: Lamb, more than almost any meat animal, varies by climate, fodder, and breed. Meat from Texas tastes different than meat from Colorado, California, or Vermont. That's because breeds are chosen depending on which animals do best in those environments.

—Tom Mylan, The Meat Hook, Brooklyn, NY

## COOKING BY THE CUT

**Best for stir-frying** leg.

**Best for panfrying** rib, loin, and shoulder chops; boneless leg strips and steaks; shoulder (burgers).

**Best for grilling** rib, loin, and shoulder chops; butterflied leg; shoulder (burgers); leg (kebabs).

**Best for roasting** boneless or bone-in leg or loin roast, rack, double-cut chops, stuffed shoulder.

**Best for braising** shoulder roasts and chops; cubed shoulder; shank; breast; neck.

## TAKE THE TEMPERATURE

The lower temperatures in each range apply to roasts, the higher temperatures to steaks and chops. Cooking lamb until well done is not recommended.

**Rare** remove from heat at 125°F (52°C); ideal temperature after resting: 132°F (56°C).

**Medium-rare** remove from heat at 130°–135°F (54°–57°C); ideal temperature after resting: 140° (60°C).

**Medium** remove from heat at 135°–140°F (57°–60°C); ideal temperature after resting: 145°F (63°C).

**Medium-well** remove from heat at 150°F (65°C); ideal temperature after resting: 160°F (71°C).

## THE CUTS

When butchered, a lamb is generally divided into five large sections, or primal cuts, as shown in the chart at right and listed below. These are each broken down into smaller retail cuts. The leg and shoulder, the more hardworking parts of the animal, are well marbled but are not as tender as the leaner loin and rib. Each part lends itself to particular cooking methods that yield the best results.

**SHOULDER** Cuts from the shoulder have more marbling than any other section. Most shoulder meat is sold as bone-in or boneless roasts and bone-in chops. A rarer cut to find is lamb shoulder ribs. The key to success with these tougher cuts is to cook them slowly using moist-heat methods such as oven or stove-top braising. The exceptions are the widely available shoulder chop, sometimes labeled "blade chop," which, especially when cut from closer to the rib, is tender enough for dry-heat cooking methods like grilling and panfrying; and a stuffed shoulder, which can be roasted in a moderate oven.

**RIB** Meat from this section is tender and juicy due to the adequate fat that keeps it from drying out during cooking. Rack of lamb and lamb rib chops are sometimes sold "frenched," with the fat and sinew removed from the bones above the eye of the meat. Some cooks prefer frenched cuts for their elegant presentation.

**LOIN** Meat of the loin section contains less marbling and is leaner than lamb from the shoulder and rib. Loin cuts are usually more affordable than rib cuts and are excellent grilled. Bone-in or boneless loin roast is a good candidate for roasting. Thinly sliced and pounded loin cuts are well suited to quick panfrying.

**LEG** The leg, with its lean meat, is the most satisfying cut to roast or grill. A bone-in leg will be tastier, but not as easy to carve. Lamb leg steaks can be broiled, grilled, or pan roasted. Boneless leg of lamb can be butterflied for even cooking and easy carving.

**BREAST AND FORELEG** Shanks, both the foreshank and hindshank, are usually braised or slow roasted so that the meat becomes tender without drying out. The high collagen content ensures creamy, falling-apart meat with rich flavor. The breast is a good-value cut that is sold either bone-in or boneless.

# LAMB CHART

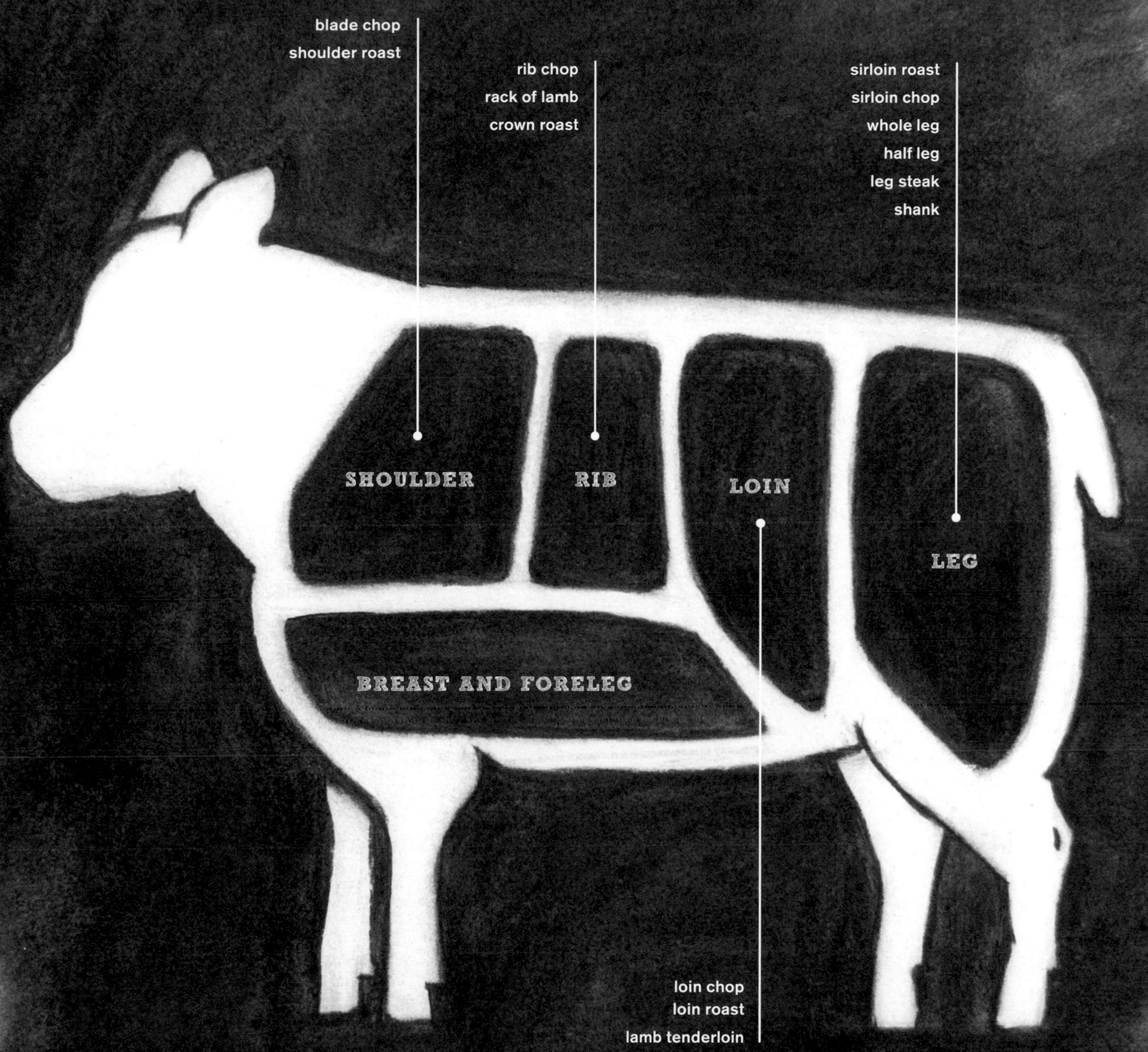
blade chop
shoulder roast
rib chop
rack of lamb
crown roast
sirloin roast
sirloin chop
whole leg
half leg
leg steak
shank
SHOULDER
RIB
LOIN
LEG
BREAST AND FORELEG
loin chop
loin roast
lamb tenderloin

## SEARED BABY LAMB CHOPS WITH FIG-BALSAMIC PAN SAUCE

 MAKES 2–4 SERVINGS

Lamb rib chops, also called "lamb lollipops" in reference to their size, are extraordinarily delicious and tender. If fresh figs are in season, incorporate a few into the sauce. During the rest of the year, dried figs, which plump up in the liquid, will work equally well. I like to serve the chops with a simple green salad, and sometimes with orzo or couscous.

Cut midway between every second bone of the rack to yield 4 double-rib chops. (Or ask your butcher to do this for you.) Pat the chops thoroughly dry and season both sides generously with salt and pepper. Let stand at room temperature for 30 minutes.

Preheat the oven to 225°F (110°C) and place a baking dish inside.

Place a large, heavy frying pan over medium-high heat, add the oil, and heat until very hot, about 2 minutes. Add the chops. Sear without moving them until golden brown, 2–2½ minutes. Turn and sear for 2–2½ minutes more. Lift each chop with tongs and sear all the fatty edges, about 1 minute total. Transfer the chops to the baking dish in the oven and continue to cook until an instant-read thermometer inserted into a chop, away from the bone, registers 135°F (57°C) for medium-rare, 20–30 minutes, or to your desired doneness (see page 144). Let rest for about 3 minutes.

Meanwhile, discard any oil from the pan, add the 2 teaspoons butter, and melt over medium-low heat. Add the prosciutto and shallots, and cook until the shallots are softened and the prosciutto is golden, about 2 minutes. Add the figs, rosemary, and vinegar, raise the heat to medium, and deglaze the pan, scraping to remove any browned bits from the bottom. Continue to cook until the liquid is reduced by about two-thirds, about 1½ minutes. Stir in the broth and a pinch of pepper. Bring to a simmer and cook for 1 minute. Remove from the heat and, if desired, stir in the cold butter until melted.

Arrange the chops on warmed plates, top with the sauce, and serve at once.

1 rack of lamb, about 2 lb (1 kg) and 8 ribs, chine bone removed, frenched, and well trimmed of fat

Kosher salt and freshly ground pepper

1 tablespoon olive oil

2 teaspoons unsalted butter

1 oz (30 g) prosciutto, finely chopped

2 large shallots, minced

4 dried figs, stems removed, finely chopped

¾ teaspoon minced fresh rosemary

⅓ cup (3 fl oz/80 ml) good-quality balsamic vinegar

1¾ cups (14 fl oz/430 ml) reduced-sodium beef broth, simmered to reduce to about ½ cup (4 fl oz/125 ml)

1 tablespoon cold unsalted butter, for finishing the sauce (optional)

---

**A NOTE FROM THE BUTCHER**

To prepare perfect rib chops, allow them to come to room temperature before searing them. Pat them dry with a paper towel prior to cooking so they will caramelize well in the pan. Once the pan is hot, sear the chops quickly, then finish them in the oven.

—Erika Nakamura, Lindy and Grundy's Meats, Los Angeles, CA

---

## PANFRIED LAMB CHOPS WITH LEMON-MINT GREMOLATA

 MAKES 2 OR 3 SERVINGS

Mint is a traditional accompaniment to lamb, but here I use it mixed with lemon zest and garlic for a modern twist. You can double the recipe if you have two very large frying pans, but don't crowd the chops into one pan. Plenty of air must circulate in order to sear the meat properly. The long resting period before finishing the dish allows the delicate chops to retain their precious juices and frees you up to make the *gremolata*.

6 single-rib lamb chops, about 2½ oz (75 g) each

1 tablespoon olive oil

1 teaspoon minced fresh rosemary

Kosher salt and freshly ground pepper

### FOR THE LEMON-MINT GREMOLATA

Grated zest of 1 lemon

1 clove garlic, minced

1 tablespoon minced fresh mint

Pat the chops dry and rub on all sides with the oil. Let stand at room temperature for 30 minutes. Rub a pinch of rosemary on both sides of each chop. Season both sides of the meaty eye of the chops lightly with salt.

Heat a large, heavy frying pan over medium-high heat until it is very hot, about 3 minutes. Add the chops without crowding them in the pan. Sear without moving them until golden, for 2 minutes. Season with salt, turn, and sear for 2 minutes more. They should be golden on both sides. Transfer the chops to a rack set over a plate and let rest, uncovered, for 30 minutes.

Meanwhile, make the *gremolata:* In a small bowl, stir together the lemon zest, garlic, and mint.

Heat the frying pan over medium-high heat. When it is hot, return the chops to the pan and reheat on each side for 30 seconds. Arrange on warmed plates, top with the *gremolata,* and serve at once.

---

### A NOTE FROM THE BUTCHER

*Merguez*, a spicy, North African lamb sausage, is a nice addition to many lamb dishes. Toss grilled and sliced *merguez* with Israeli couscous and the *gremolata* used in this recipe for a quick salad. *Merguez* can also be used in stuffings for meat with great results.

—Greg Westergreen, Clancey's Meats and Fish, Minneapolis, MN

---

Tender lamb mixes with earthy *farro*, sweet pomegranate seeds, aromatic mint, and crunchy fennel in this main-course salad, which I like to serve at the first sign of spring. Lamb tenderloin is an extremely tender cut—almost like butter—but because of its small size, care must be taken not to overcook it. It is a special-order item in most butcher shops, but is well worth seeking out.

Place the *farro* in a saucepan and add cold water to cover by 2 inches (5 cm). Bring to a rapid boil over high heat and cook for 5 minutes. Remove from the heat and let stand, covered, until plump and al dente, 45–50 minutes. Drain, shaking off as much excess water as possible. Set aside. The *farro* may be refrigerated for up to 2 days; bring to room temperature before serving.

Brush the lamb on all sides with 2 tablespoons of the oil. Season generously with salt, pepper, and the rosemary, rubbing the rosemary on all sides of the tenderloins. Let stand at room temperature for about 1 hour.

In a large bowl, whisk together the vinegar, lemon juice, and the remaining 3 tablespoons oil. Add ½ teaspoon salt and ¼ teaspoon pepper. Stir in the *farro* and fennel. Refrigerate until serving.

Prepare a charcoal or gas grill for direct-heat grilling over medium-high heat, or preheat a cast-iron stove-top grill pan over medium-high heat. Place the tenderloins on the grill rack over the hottest part of the fire or in the grill pan, and cook until dark brown, 3–4 minutes. Turn and cook until lightly brown, just 2 minutes more, to avoid overcooking. Transfer the lamb to a cutting board and let rest for 5 minutes.

Cut the tenderloins across the grain on the diagonal into slices about ½ inch (12 mm) thick. Arrange on the salad, garnish with the mint and pomegranate seeds, and serve at once.

Note: To substitute bulgur, place 1 cup (6 oz/185 g) medium-grind bulgur in a heatproof bowl and add 2 cups (16 fl oz/500 ml) boiling water. Let stand for 30 minutes, then fluff with a fork.

1 cup (8 oz/250 g) farro (see note)

4 lamb tenderloins, about 1 lb (500 g) total weight, and each 4–6 inches (10–15 cm) long, silverskin removed

5 tablespoons (3 fl oz/80 ml) olive oil

Kosher salt and freshly ground pepper

1 tablespoon minced fresh rosemary

2 teaspoons balsamic vinegar

2 tablespoons fresh lemon juice

1 fennel bulb, trimmed, quartered, and cored, then thinly shaved crosswise

¼ cup (⅓ oz/10 g) fresh mint leaves

½ cup (2 oz/60 g) pomegranate seeds

## STIR-FRIED LAMB WITH BROCCOLI AND MUSHROOMS

 MAKES 4 SERVINGS

1 lb (500 g) broccoli

1 lb (500 g) boneless lamb leg steaks

Kosher salt and freshly ground pepper

2 tablespoons oyster sauce

1 tablespoon reduced-sodium chicken or vegetable broth

1½ teaspoons Thai or Vietnamese fish sauce

1½ teaspoons Asian sesame oil

1½ teaspoons rice vinegar

3 tablespoons peanut or canola oil

4 cloves garlic, thinly sliced

½ lb (250 g) cremini or button mushrooms, brushed clean and cut into slices about ¼ inch (6 mm) thick

1 lime, cut into 6 wedges

1½ tablespoons coarsely chopped fresh mint

If you don't have a wok or very large frying pan, cook the lamb in two batches to avoid crowding the pan. Don't use a nonstick pan, though, or you won't achieve the same rich, caramelized flavor. Add a little more oil before stir-frying the second batch, if necessary, and be sure the pan is hot before adding the meat.

Separate the broccoli florets from the stems and cut the florets into 1-inch (2.5-cm) pieces. Peel the stems with a vegetable peeler and cut on the diagonal into slices ¼ inch (6 mm) thick.

Place the lamb on a baking sheet and freeze, uncovered, for 15 minutes. Cut into strips about 1½ inches (4 cm) long, ¾ inch (2 cm) wide, and ½ inch (12 mm) thick. Season generously with salt and pepper.

In a bowl, stir together the oyster sauce, broth, fish sauce, sesame oil, and vinegar. Set aside.

Heat 1 tablespoon of the peanut oil in a large frying pan or wok over high heat until it is very hot, 2–3 minutes. Add the lamb, distributing it evenly, and cook without moving it for about 20 seconds. Continue to cook the lamb, tossing and stirring it every 15–20 seconds, until browned, about 3 minutes more. Transfer to a platter.

Add the remaining 2 tablespoons peanut oil to the pan and heat until very hot. Add the garlic and mushrooms and toss and stir for 1 minute. Add the broccoli and cook, tossing and stirring every 15–20 seconds, until slightly softened, 2–3 minutes. Return the lamb to the pan and add the oyster sauce mixture. Reduce the heat to medium and toss for 1–2 minutes to blend the flavors and warm through.

Transfer to a platter and squeeze 2 lime wedges over the top. Garnish with the mint and serve at once. Pass the remaining lime wedges at the table.

Stand by your grill for the entire cooking time, because these little chops will cook fast. If you don't have a reliable thermometer, look at the color of the chops—they should be ready when the second side is golden brown. When pressed, the meat should yield slightly, rather than be firm.

In a shallow nonreactive dish large enough to hold the chops in one layer, whisk together the lemon zest and juice, the garlic, and 1 tablespoon of the oil. Add the lamb, turn once, and let stand for 15 minutes. Turn and let stand for 15 minutes more.

Meanwhile, if using fresh peas, prepare an ice bath. Bring a pot of lightly salted water to a rapid boil. Add the peas and cook until not quite tender, 1–2 minutes. Immediately drain and transfer to the ice bath to stop the cooking. Drain well and spread on a clean towel to remove excess moisture. If using thawed frozen peas, roll around gently on a towel to dry.

In a bowl, combine the peas, the remaining 2 tablespoons olive oil, and the mint. Add ½ teaspoon salt and season with pepper. Toss gently.

Prepare a charcoal or gas grill for direct-heat grilling over high heat. If using charcoal, spread the coals evenly so there are no hot spots. Blot the chops with paper towels and season both sides generously with salt. Place on the grill rack, and after about 2 minutes, check the color of the undersides. When they are dark brown and sizzling but not blackening, turn the chops. Depending on how hot your grill gets, this will take 2–5 minutes. Continue to cook until an instant-read thermometer inserted into a chop away from the bone registers 135°F (57°C) for medium-rare, or to your desired doneness (see page 144). Transfer to a platter, season with pepper, and let rest for 5–10 minutes.

Fold the vinegar and feta into the salad. Serve at once alongside the chops.

# GRILLED BABY LAMB CHOPS WITH PEA, FETA, AND MINT SALAD

 MAKES 4 SERVINGS

Grated zest of 1 lemon, plus 2 tablespoons juice

2 large cloves garlic, minced

3 tablespoons olive oil

8 single-rib lamb chops, 4–5 oz (125–155 g) and 1–1¼ inches (2.5–3 cm) thick

Ice cubes

3 cups (15 oz/470 g) shelled English peas or thawed frozen petite peas

2 tablespoons minced fresh mint

Kosher salt and freshly ground pepper

1 tablespoon red wine vinegar

3 oz (90 g) mild feta cheese, preferably French, crumbled

---

**A NOTE FROM THE BUTCHER**

Don't let the butcher cut the chops on the saw. Instead, ask him or her to remove the backbone and the chine bone and then slice between the ribs with a knife. Be sure the rib bones are at least 6 inches (15 cm) long so you can french them—that is, remove all the gristly meat and fat along their length.

—Mark Martin, Nelson's Meat Market, Cedar Rapids, IA

---

This Middle East–inspired dish features an enticing array of seasonings and textures. The saltiness of the *anchoïade* tames the richness of the lamb, and the yogurt brightens up everything. When meat is ground for burgers, the goal is to keep it crumbly and loose. Here, you want to grind the meat until it is very smooth, and then compress it firmly around the skewers. You can also ask your butcher to finely grind the meat for you.

## LAMB KOFTA WITH ANCHOÏADE AND MINT YOGURT

 MAKES 4 SERVINGS

Cut the meat into rough 1-inch (2.5-cm) chunks. Remove the large, hard pockets of fat, but retain some fat, which will help keep the meat juicy. Place the lamb on a baking sheet and freeze, uncovered, for 20 minutes.

Brush the onion slices very lightly with oil. Heat a cast-iron frying pan or grill pan over medium-high heat. Add the onion slices and cook, turning, until charred and slightly wilted, about 5 minutes. Let cool.

Place half of the lamb in a food processor and pulse about 15 times until minced. You may have to redistribute the meat to achieve an even texture. Transfer to a large bowl, process the remaining lamb, and add to the bowl. Add the grilled onion, dill, paprika, cumin, cinnamon, chile powder, and 1 teaspoon salt to the processor and pulse until finely minced. Transfer to the bowl. With clean hands, combine all the ingredients evenly. Refrigerate for 30 minutes. If using bamboo skewers, soak 8 skewers in water for at least 30 minutes.

Meanwhile, make the *anchoïade*: In a mini food processor, combine the anchovies, garlic, and parsley. Season with pepper. Add just enough oil to moisten the ingredients and pulse until smooth.

Divide the lamb mixture into 8 equal portions. With wet hands, form a sausage shape 4–5 inches (10–13 cm) long and about 1½ inches (4 cm) in diameter around each skewer, molding and compressing the mixture firmly and evenly and pressing it at either end. Wrap 2 inches (5 cm) of the blunt end of each skewer in aluminum foil to make a handle. Brush the lamb mixture lightly with oil and season generously with pepper.

Preheat a charcoal or gas grill for direct-heat grilling over high heat. Oil the grill rack well. Place the skewers on the grill rack over the hottest part of the fire and cook, turning once or twice, until the exterior is golden brown, about 10 minutes. Transfer to a platter and let rest for 2 minutes.

Make the mint yogurt: In a small bowl, stir together the yogurt, vinegar, mint, and ¼ teaspoon salt. Remove the foil from the skewers and arrange on warmed plates. Drizzle with the *anchoïade* and serve at once with the mint yogurt.

1¼ lb (625 g) boneless lamb shoulder

1 small yellow onion, cut into slices ½ inch (12 mm) thick

Olive oil for brushing

3 tablespoons minced fresh dill

1 tablespoon sweet paprika

2 teaspoons ground cumin

¾ teaspoon ground cinnamon

½ teaspoon mild chile powder

Kosher salt and freshly ground pepper

**FOR THE ANCHOÏADE**

12 anchovy fillets, soaked in water for 5 minutes, drained, and patted dry

2 cloves garlic, thinly sliced

1½ teaspoons coarsely chopped fresh flat-leaf parsley

Freshly ground pepper

3–4 tablespoons extra-virgin olive oil

**FOR THE MINT YOGURT**

¾ cup (6 oz/185 g) plain Greek yogurt

2 tablespoons white wine vinegar

1 tablespoon minced fresh mint

Kosher salt

# PAN-ROASTED T-BONE CHOPS WITH SALSA VERDE

 MAKES 4 SERVINGS

Lamb loin chops vary in size. Count on 2 chops per person for light eaters and 3 chops for diners with heartier appetites. Make the salsa verde no more than 3 to 4 hours in advance for the most vibrant color. If that's not possible, the sauce can be tightly covered and refrigerated for up to 12 hours.

## FOR THE SALSA VERDE

1 clove garlic

1 anchovy fillet, soaked in warm water for 5 minutes, drained, and patted dry

1¼ cups (1½ oz/45 g) firmly packed fresh flat-leaf parsley leaves

¼ cup (¼ oz/7 g) packed fresh mint leaves

1 tablespoon capers, rinsed

1 teaspoon Dijon mustard

1½ teaspoons white or red wine vinegar

⅓ cup (3 fl oz/80 ml) extra-virgin olive oil

8–12 bone-in T-bone or loin lamb chops, 2–2½ lb (1–1.25 kg) total weight, each about 1½ inches (4 cm) thick

Kosher salt and freshly ground pepper

2 teaspoons olive oil

2 teaspoons unsalted butter

To make the *salsa verde*, in a mini food processor, pulse the garlic until minced. Add the anchovy, parsley, mint, capers, mustard, and vinegar. Pulse until smooth. Add the oil and pulse until evenly blended and thick. Cover and refrigerate for at least 1 hour to blend the flavors.

Remove the chops from the refrigerator and let stand at room temperature for 30 minutes. Preheat the oven to 250°F (120°C). Pat the chops dry with paper towels and season both sides generously with salt and pepper.

Place a large ovenproof frying pan over high heat, add the oil, and heat until it begins to shimmer, about 3 minutes. Add the butter and reduce the heat to medium-high. When the butter foams, add the chops without letting them touch. Sear without moving them until crusty and golden, 2–2½ minutes. Turn and sear for 2 minutes more. Lift each chop with tongs and sear all the fatty edges, about 45 seconds per chop.

Transfer the pan to the oven and cook the chops until an instant-read thermometer inserted into a chop, away from the bone, registers 135°F (57°C) for medium-rare, 20–25 minutes, or to your desired doneness (see page 144). Transfer to a platter and let rest for about 5 minutes. Top with the *salsa verde* and serve at once.

### A NOTE FROM THE BUTCHER

When you cook bone-in chops, you will often find that even though the meaty part is perfectly cooked, a pocket of meat next to the bone remains raw. To avoid this, stand the chop on the flat part of the bone in the pan or on the grill. This allows the bone to start heating up first, which helps the meat near it to cook more evenly.

—Benjamin Dyer, Laurelhurst Market, Portland, OR

## LAMB AND ARTICHOKE SPIEDINI WITH OREGANO POLENTA

**MAKES 4–6 SERVINGS**

*Spiedini* are the Italian version of skewered meat. This combination of lamb and artichoke hearts is easy to assemble, yet sophisticated enough for any occasion. It's not crucial that the artichoke hearts be completely thawed before they are marinated, because they will finish thawing while they soak.

In a bowl, combine the lamb, artichokes, lemon zest and juice, 3 tablespoons oil, garlic, and oregano. Add ½ teaspoon salt and season with pepper. Toss to combine and let stand at room temperature for 1 hour, or cover and refrigerate for at least 2 hours or up to 6 hours. Toss the mixture occasionally. If using bamboo skewers, soak 14 skewers in water for 30–40 minutes.

Meanwhile, to prepare the polenta, heat a small amount of oil in a heavy saucepan over low heat. Add the garlic, and before it has a chance to scorch, stir in the oregano and cook, stirring, for 30 seconds. Add a mixture of half milk and half broth in place of the quantity of water called for in the recipe on the polenta box. Bring to a boil and cook the polenta according to the package instructions. Just before the polenta is done, stir in the Parmesan and butter. Cover and hold in a warm place, or keep warm in the top of a double boiler over barely simmering water.

Prepare a charcoal or gas grill for direct-heat grilling over medium-high heat, or preheat a large cast-iron stove-top grill pan over medium-high heat. Thread the ingredients onto each skewer in the following order: 1 artichoke heart, 2 lamb pieces, 1 artichoke heart, 2 lamb pieces, and 1 artichoke heart. Position them close to the pointed end of the skewer, and press the lamb pieces snugly together. Wrap about 2 inches (5 cm) of the blunt end of each skewer with aluminum foil to make a handle.

Place the skewers on the grill rack over the hottest part of the fire or in the grill pan, and cook until browned, about 2½ minutes. Turn and cook until browned and just firm to the touch, 2–3 minutes more.

Remove the foil from the skewers and arrange on a warmed platter. Season with salt and garnish with lemon wedges. Serve at once with the hot polenta.

1¼ lb (625 g) boneless lamb leg steaks, trimmed of excess fat and gristle and cut into ¾-inch (2-cm) cubes

1 lb (500 g) thawed frozen artichoke hearts

Grated zest and juice of 1 lemon

3 tablespoons olive oil, plus extra for brushing

2 cloves garlic, minced

2 teaspoons minced fresh oregano

Kosher salt and freshly ground pepper

Lemon wedges for serving

### FOR THE OREGANO POLENTA

Olive oil

2 cloves garlic

1 tablespoon minced fresh oregano

Whole milk as needed

Reduced-sodium chicken broth as needed

1 box (9 oz/280 g) instant polenta

2 tablespoons grated Parmesan cheese

2 tablespoons unsalted butter

## LAMB AND PITA SALAD

MAKES 4–6 SERVINGS

This salad is similar to *fattoush*, a Middle Eastern favorite that uses a sweet-and-savory combination of flavors. It is worth seeking out sumac (an aromatic spice) and *za'atar* (a spice blend) at a well-stocked supermarket or Middle Eastern store to impart an authentic flavor to the salad. Pomegranate molasses varies in sweetness; taste the dressing first and add honey until the sourness of the molasses is tamed.

1¼ lb (625 g) boneless lamb leg steaks, each about ½ inch (12 mm) thick, or 1½ lb (750 g) bone-in lamb leg steaks

2 tablespoons olive oil

½ teaspoon ground cumin

Kosher salt and freshly ground pepper

### FOR THE PITA SALAD

2 pita breads, split horizontally

2 cloves garlic

2 tablespoons fresh lemon juice

2 teaspoons pomegranate molasses

2–3 teaspoons honey

¼ cup (2 fl oz/60 ml) extra-virgin olive oil

Kosher salt

2 large tomatoes, halved crosswise, seeded, and diced

4 green onions, white and light green parts, thinly sliced

1 English cucumber, seeded and cut into small dice

4–6 radishes, coarsely chopped

1 head romaine lettuce, pale inner leaves only, cut crosswise into ½-inch (12-mm) pieces

½ cup (½ oz/15 g) coarsely chopped fresh flat-leaf parsley

½ cup (¾ oz/20 g) coarsely chopped fresh mint

1 tablespoon ground sumac or *za'atar*

Brush both sides of the lamb steaks with oil and season with the cumin and generously with salt and pepper. Let stand at room temperature for about 1 hour.

To make the pita salad, preheat the oven to 350°F (180°C). Arrange the pita breads on a baking sheet and bake until lightly crisped and golden, about 10 minutes. Let cool, then break into 1-inch (2.5-cm) pieces. In a mini food processor, process the garlic until minced. Add the lemon juice, molasses, honey, oil, and 1 teaspoon salt. Pulse to combine. Set the pita pieces and dressing aside. In a large serving bowl, combine the tomatoes, green onions, cucumber, radishes, romaine, parsley, and mint. Toss to combine. Refrigerate while you cook the lamb.

Prepare a charcoal or gas grill for direct-heat grilling over high heat, or preheat a cast-iron stove-top grill pan over high heat. Place the steaks on the grill rack over the hottest part of the fire or in the grill pan, and cook, turning once, until an instant-read thermometer inserted into a steak registers 135°F (57°C) for medium-rare, 2–2½ minutes per side, or to your desired doneness (see page 144). Transfer to a cutting board and let rest for 5 minutes. Cut the steaks crosswise into strips 1 inch (2.5 cm) wide, working around the bone if necessary.

Add the pita pieces to the salad, drizzle with the dressing, and toss to mix. Arrange the lamb on top, sprinkle with the sumac, and serve at once.

Burgers are often thought of as casual fare, but I like to dress up these lamb burgers by serving them without the buns, placing them instead on a bed of grilled vegetables, and accompanying them with *tzatziki*, a tangy Greek yogurt-based sauce. Eggplant or red peppers could be swapped in for the zucchini. Use a restrained hand when forming the burgers. A gentle touch ensures that they will be light and tender.

In a frying pan over medium-low heat, warm the 2 tablespoons oil. Add the onion and cook, stirring occasionally, until very soft, about 6 minutes. Transfer to a large bowl and let cool for 5 minutes. Add the dill, bread crumbs, cumin, garlic, and lamb. Add ¾ teaspoon salt and season with pepper. Using a fork, blend the ingredients evenly. With a light hand, form 4 loosely packed patties, then gently flatten them to about ¾ inch (2 cm) thick. Refrigerate for at least 1 hour or up to 4 hours. Cover with plastic wrap if chilling for more than 1 hour.

In a bowl, toss the zucchini with just enough oil to lightly coat all sides. Season with salt and pepper. Set aside.

To make the *tzatziki*, in a bowl, whisk together the yogurt, vinegar, cucumber, dill, and garlic. Whisk in ¼ teaspoon salt. Taste and adjust the seasoning, adding more salt or vinegar if desired.

Remove the burgers from the refrigerator. Prepare a charcoal or gas grill for direct-heat grilling over medium-high heat, or preheat a cast-iron stove-top grill pan over medium-high heat. Oil the grill rack well. Brush the tops of the burgers lightly with oil and season generously with salt and pepper. Place the burgers, oiled side down, on the grill rack over the hottest part of the fire or in the grill pan, and cook for 3 minutes. Brush the burgers with oil and season with salt and pepper, turn, and cook until an instant-read thermometer inserted into a burger registers 135°F (57°C) for medium-rare, 3–7 minutes, or to your desired doneness (see page 144). Transfer to a platter and let rest, loosely covered with aluminum foil, for 5 minutes.

Place the zucchini slices on the grill rack or in the grill pan, and cook, turning once, until golden, tender, and lightly charred, about 5 minutes.

Arrange the zucchini slices on plates. Top with the burgers, garnish with the *tzatziki*, and serve at once.

2 tablespoons olive oil, plus more for coating

1 small yellow onion, very finely chopped

¼ cup (⅓ oz/10 g) minced fresh dill

1 tablespoon fine dried bread crumbs

1¼ teaspoons ground cumin

3 large cloves garlic, minced

1¼ lb (625 g) coarsely ground lamb, preferably from the shoulder

Kosher salt and freshly ground pepper

4 small zucchini, cut lengthwise into slices about ⅓ inch (9 mm) thick

**FOR THE TZATZIKI**

1½ cups (12 oz/375 g) plain Greek yogurt

2 tablespoons white wine vinegar

½ English cucumber, peeled, seeded, and finely grated

1 tablespoon minced fresh dill

1 large clove garlic, minced

---

🔪 **A NOTE FROM THE BUTCHER**

Ask your butcher for ground lamb with only 10 percent fat. Too much lamb fat gives burgers a gamy taste that some people don't like.

—James Cross, Marczyk Fine Foods, Denver, CO

---

Wrapping meat in aluminum foil and roasting it slowly in the oven is similar to braising. The steam trapped in the foil packet envelops the meat and keeps it moist during the long roasting. Take your time when searing the lamb shanks so that they develop a golden crust. I like to serve the shanks with couscous and a simple green salad.

## BAKED LAMB SHANKS WITH FENNEL GREMOLATA

 MAKES 4–6 SERVINGS

Preheat the oven to 325°F (165°C) and place a rimmed baking sheet inside.

In a mini food processor or with a sharp knife, chop the garlic, anchovies (if using), shallots, and rosemary. Transfer to a bowl, add ¼ teaspoon salt (or ½ teaspoon salt if not using the anchovies), and season with pepper. Add 2 tablespoons of the wine, 3 tablespoons of the oil, and the lemon zest and juice. Mix until thin paste forms.

Place a large, heavy frying pan over medium heat and add the remaining 1 tablespoon oil. Pat the lamb shanks dry and season generously with salt and pepper on all sides. When the oil begins to shimmer, sear 2 of the shanks until golden brown on all sides, about 8 minutes per side. Transfer to a platter and sear the remaining shanks. Pour off the fat from the pan, add the remaining 1 tablespoon wine, and quickly deglaze the pan, stirring to scrape the browned bits from the bottom. Add to the paste.

Place 4 large squares of heavy-duty aluminum foil on a work surface. Set a shank in the center of each, pull up the sides of the foil slightly, and divide the flavoring paste evenly among the packets, dolloping the mixture on top of the shanks. Crimp the foil firmly to seal the packets thoroughly. Transfer to the baking sheet in the oven and cook, turning the packets every 30 minutes or so, until the shanks are very tender, 2–2¼ hours.

Meanwhile, prepare the *gremolata:* In a small bowl, stir together the fennel fronds, chopped fennel, and orange zest.

Carefully open the packets and transfer the lamb shanks to a warmed platter. Pour the juices from the packets into a large glass measuring pitcher and let settle for 1 minute. With a bulb baster, remove some of the juices from underneath the fat, and use as much as you like to moisten the lamb shanks. Garnish with the *gremolata* and serve at once.

20 cloves garlic

6 small anchovy fillets (optional)

2 shallots, halved

2 large sprigs rosemary

Kosher salt and freshly ground pepper

3 tablespoons dry white wine or vermouth

4 tablespoons (2 fl oz/60 ml) extra-virgin olive oil

Grated zest of 1 lemon

2 teaspoons fresh lemon juice

4 meaty lamb shanks, about 1 lb (500 g) each

### FOR THE FENNEL GREMOLATA

2 tablespoons minced fennel fronds or fresh dill

2 tablespoons finely chopped fennel

Grated zest of 1 orange

# GRILLED LEG OF LAMB WITH LIME-CHIVE CRÈME FRAÎCHE

 MAKES 6 SERVINGS

Leg of lamb is often roasted, but grilling gives this tender cut a crispy exterior while leaving the interior juicy and rosy. Butterflying the leg creates an uneven surface that nicely traps the olive oil and seasoning that I rub over it. Serve the lamb alongside grilled asparagus for a springtime feast.

1 leg of lamb, about 5 lb (2.5 kg), butterflied, flattened, and trimmed of excess fat

Olive oil for coating

1 teaspoon dried thyme

1½ lb (750 g) asparagus spears

Kosher salt and freshly ground pepper

1 cup (8 oz/250 g) crème fraîche

Grated zest of 1 lime

4 teaspoons fresh lime juice

1 tablespoon finely snipped fresh chives

Place the lamb on a rimmed platter or in a baking dish. Rub generously all over with oil and then with the thyme, working it into all the nooks and crannies. Let stand at room temperature for about 30 minutes.

Snap off the bottom ends of the asparagus spears 1–1½ inches (2.5–4 cm) above the base. Peel the bottom 2 inches (5 cm) of the spears with a vegetable peeler. This helps the spears cook evenly and gives them a luminous jade-green color.

Prepare a gas or charcoal grill for direct-heat cooking over medium-high heat. Season both sides of the lamb generously with salt and pepper. If using a gas grill, reduce the heat to medium; if using a charcoal grill, raise the grill rack. Place the lamb on the grill rack with the uneven side down and grill for 15 minutes. Move the lamb if there are excessive flare-ups; a little flame is fine. Turn the lamb and grill until an instant-read thermometer inserted into the lamb at the thickest point registers 125°F–130°F (52°C–54°C), 15–20 minutes more. Because of the irregular thickness of the meat, some parts will be rare and others well done. Transfer to a platter, tent loosely with aluminum foil, and let rest for 10–15 minutes.

Place the asparagus spears perpendicular to the bars of the grill rack and cook, turning, until golden brown but not scorched and just tender, 4–8 minutes.

In a bowl, stir together the crème fraîche, lime zest and juice, and chives. Add ½ teaspoon salt and season with pepper.

Cut the lamb across the grain into thin slices. Arrange on a warmed platter with the asparagus. Serve at once with the lime-chive crème fraîche.

## A NOTE FROM THE BUTCHER

If you're serving six people or fewer, you can get by with three-quarters or one-half of a leg of lamb. Since the meat is being grilled, ask for the butt or sirloin half. The meat at this end is more tender than the shank end when grilled. If boning and butterflying the meat at home, cover it with plastic wrap and give it a whack or two with your kid's baseball bat to flatten it out. It's a good release after a hard day!

—Don Kuzaro, Jr., Don & Joe's Meats, Seattle, WA

Rack of lamb is a luxurious and tasty cut: the meat stays tender when cooked as part of a roast, and the chops can be carved at the table for an elegant presentation. The stuffing in this recipe—a mix of dried cranberries, dates, and almonds—reminds me of fall. Accompany the lamb with herb-roasted potatoes.

Rub the lamb all over with oil and then with the thyme, rosemary, and 1 teaspoon pepper. Cover and refrigerate for at least 2 hours or preferably up to 12 hours. Let stand at room temperature for 1 hour.

To make the stuffing, place the cranberries in a small saucepan and barely cover with water. Add the sherry. Bring to a simmer, remove from the heat, and let stand for 10 minutes. Drain well. In a mini food processor, pulse the almonds for 2 seconds. Add the cranberries, dates, mint, butter, and bread crumbs. Add ½ teaspoon salt and season with pepper. Pulse to form a slightly chunky paste.

Preheat the oven to 400°F (200°C) and place a large roasting pan inside. Using a long, thin knife, such as a carving knife, cut a 2-inch (5-cm) slit all the way through each rack, right in the center, or eye, of the meat. Widen the slit with the handle of a wooden spoon. Poke about one-fourth of the stuffing into the slit from either end of each rack, pushing the stuffing with the spoon handle. Season the racks generously with salt and pepper.

Place both racks, rounded (fat) side down, in the pan, and roast for 10 minutes. Turn and roast until an instant-read thermometer inserted into the meat, not the stuffing, near the center registers 135°F (57°C) for medium-rare, 12–15 minutes more, or to your desired doneness (see page 144). Transfer to a cutting board, tent loosely with aluminum foil, and let rest for 5–10 minutes. Carve into individual chops and serve.

2 racks of lamb, 1–1¼ lb (500–625 g) each, chine bone removed, frenched, and well trimmed of fat

Olive oil for coating

1 teaspoon chopped fresh thyme

1 teaspoon minced fresh rosemary

Kosher salt and freshly ground pepper

**FOR THE STUFFING**

½ cup (2 oz/60 g) dried cranberries

2 tablespoons medium-dry sherry

¼ cup (1 oz/30 g) almonds

5 dates, coarsely chopped

1 tablespoon coarsely chopped fresh mint or flat-leaf parsley

2 tablespoons unsalted butter, at room temperature

¼ cup (½ oz/15 g) fresh bread crumbs

Kosher salt and freshly ground pepper

---

### A NOTE FROM THE BUTCHER

A rack can be frenched, exposing the tips of the bones. This is a beautiful presentation, but I like the flavorful meat between the bones! An experienced butcher will know how to skillfully trim the fat from the rack. This will eliminate the gamy flavor that many people associate with lamb.

—Ron Savenor, Savenor's Market, Boston, MA

---

# LAMB CURRY WITH SQUASH, CHICKPEAS, AND APRICOTS

 MAKES 6 SERVINGS

For this colorful take on a classic curry, lamb shoulder is braised on the stove top, resulting in juicy and flavorful meat. Do not be in a hurry when browning the meat before the braising begins, and resist the urge to turn the cubes too frequently, since the goal is to caramelize the exterior. Serve the curry in wide bowls over couscous to soak up the silky coconut-based sauce.

⅓ cup (1 oz/30 g) Madras curry powder

2 teaspoons plus 2½ tablespoons canola oil

½ cup (2½ oz/75 g) slivered almonds

1 large yellow onion, thinly sliced

5 cloves garlic, thinly sliced

Kosher salt and freshly ground pepper

1¾–2 lb (875 g–1 kg) well-trimmed boneless lamb shoulder, cut into 1-inch (2.5-cm) cubes

1 cup (7 oz/220 g) crushed tomatoes

2½ tablespoons reduced-sodium soy sauce

1 can (15 oz/470 g) chickpeas, rinsed and drained

¾ lb (375 g) yellow squash, cut into ½-inch (12-mm) cubes

1½ cups (12 fl oz/375 ml) unsweetened coconut milk

1 cup (6 oz/185 g) dried apricots, diced

1 tablespoon fresh mint or cilantro leaves

In a small bowl, whisk the curry powder with ⅓ cup (3 fl oz/80 ml) water to make a paste. Set aside.

Place a large frying pan over medium heat and add the 2 teaspoons oil. Add the almonds and sauté, shaking the pan constantly as soon as they begin to sizzle, until golden brown, 1–2 minutes. Using a slotted spoon, transfer the almonds to a bowl.

Add 1½ tablespoons of the remaining oil to the pan. When it is hot, add the onion and cook, stirring occasionally, until softened and golden, 8–10 minutes. Stir in the garlic and a scant ½ teaspoon salt, and cook for 1 minute more. Remove from the heat. With the slotted spoon, transfer the onion and garlic to a food processor. Purée until thick and almost smooth.

Pat the lamb thoroughly dry and season it generously with salt and pepper. Place the frying pan over medium-high heat and add the remaining 1 tablespoon oil. Add half of the lamb cubes and sear, turning with tongs, until golden on all sides, about 5 minutes. Transfer to a plate and sear the remaining lamb. Reduce the heat to low, return the lamb to the pan, add the curry paste, and stir to glaze the lamb with the paste. Add the puréed onion-garlic mixture, tomatoes, soy sauce, and a pinch of pepper. Cover the pan and adjust the heat so that the mixture simmers very gently for 15 minutes. Add the chickpeas, squash, and coconut milk and cook, stirring occasionally, for 15 minutes. Stir in the apricots and cook for 15 minutes more.

Spoon into warmed bowls, garnish with the toasted almonds and mint, and serve at once.

After several hours of roasting and then braising in the oven, this lamb is so tender that when cut or shredded it's almost like a ragout sauce. One way to serve the meat is to shred it and add it to cooked fettuccine that has been lightly tossed with butter. This lamb is very forgiving: it is ready to eat straight from the oven, or it can be set aside for up to 1 hour, then rewarmed in a low oven.

## SLOW-ROASTED LEG OF LAMB WITH ORANGE-TAPENADE AIOLI

 MAKES 6 OR 7 SERVINGS

With a small, sharp knife, cut slits all over the lamb and poke garlic slivers into the slits. Let the lamb stand at room temperature for about 1½ hours.

Preheat the oven to 450°F (230°C). Rub the lamb all over with oil. Season generously with salt and pepper, and then rub with the thyme.

Place the leg, fat side down, in a large roasting pan. Roast for 15 minutes. Add the whole garlic cloves, onion, carrots, and celery to the pan. Turn the lamb, making sure that some of the vegetables are underneath it. Continue to roast for 15 minutes. Reduce the oven temperature to 300°F (150°C), cover tightly with aluminum foil, and roast for 3 hours.

In a small bowl, stir together the tomato paste, wine, broth, and vinegar. Uncover the pan, turn the lamb, and toss the bay leaves over the vegetables. Spoon about ½ cup (4 fl oz/125 ml) of the wine mixture over the lamb. Continue to roast, uncovered, for 2 hours more, drizzling ½ cup of the wine mixture over the lamb every 20–30 minutes, until all the mixture is used. Turn the lamb after 1 hour. The lamb is ready when it is very tender and almost falling apart (or falling off the bone if using a bone-in leg of lamb). Gently transfer the lamb to a warmed platter and tent loosely with aluminum foil.

Pour the pan juices and vegetables into a large fine-mesh sieve placed over a large measuring pitcher. Press down hard on the vegetables to extract all the juices. Discard the vegetables. Let the juices stand for 1 minute, then spoon off the fat. Warm the juices, if necessary.

Snip the strings from the lamb. Shred the lamb, discarding the bone if necessary. Serve at once, drizzled with the pan juices.

1 boneless or bone-in leg of lamb, 5½–7 lb (2.75–3.5 kg), trimmed of excess fat and tied by the butcher if boneless

2 heads garlic, 4 cloves slivered, the rest left whole

Olive oil

Kosher salt and freshly ground pepper

2 teaspoons dried thyme

1 large yellow onion, coarsely chopped

3 carrots, peeled and coarsely chopped

3 ribs celery, coarsely chopped

2 tablespoons tomato paste

1 cup (8 fl oz/250 ml) fruity red wine, such as Zinfandel

1 cup (8 fl oz/250 ml) reduced-sodium chicken broth

⅓ cup (3 fl oz/80 ml) red wine vinegar

3 bay leaves

Orange-Tapenade Aioli (page 213)

---

**A NOTE FROM THE BUTCHER**

Seek out a leg of lamb with the shank still attached. Ask the butcher to trim it off, then roast it separately with the garlic, onions, and carrots and use it to flavor vegetable-barley soup.

—James Cross, Marczyk Fine Foods, Denver, CO

---

Lamb shoulder chops are much less expensive than loin or rib chops, and because they have many more bones, they are far more flavorful as well. You would not want to braise the pricier, smaller loin or rib chops—which are best served rosy and pink—but shoulder chops develop an irresistible richness after simmering in a rich red-wine broth.

Season both sides of the chops generously with salt and pepper. Place a large, heavy frying pan over medium-high heat and add 1 tablespoon of the oil. When the oil begins to shimmer, add the chops without crowding them in the pan, and sear for 2–2½ minutes. Turn and sear for 2–2½ minutes more. Transfer to a platter.

Pour off the fat from the pan and reduce the heat to medium-low; wait for about 1 minute for the pan to cool down. Add the remaining 1 tablespoon oil. Add the shallots and cook until softened, about 5 minutes. Add the garlic and rosemary and cook, stirring, for 1 minute more. Add the wine and deglaze the pan, stirring to remove the browned bits from the bottom. Simmer the liquid until reduced by about half, about 2 minutes.

Stir in the tomatoes and their juices and the olives. Return the chops to the pan, reduce the heat to low, cover, and simmer gently until the chops are tender and still slightly pink at the center and an instant-read thermometer inserted into a chop, away from the bone, registers 135°–145°F (57°–63°C), or to desired doneness (page 144), about 15 minutes. Turn and redistribute the chops halfway through. Transfer the chops to warmed plates.

Raise the heat to high and simmer briskly until the braising juices are slightly thickened, 3–4 minutes. Taste and adjust the seasoning. Stir in the parsley. Spoon the sauce over the chops and serve at once.

# BRAISED LAMB SHOULDER CHOPS WITH TOMATOES AND ROSEMARY

 MAKES 4 SERVINGS

4 lamb shoulder chops, each 10–12 oz (315–375 g) and ¾ inch (2 cm) thick, trimmed of excess fat

Kosher salt and freshly ground pepper

2 tablespoons olive oil

2 large shallots, finely chopped

3 cloves garlic, minced

1 tablespoon minced fresh rosemary

⅓ cup (3 fl oz/80 ml) dry red wine

5 canned tomatoes, preferably San Marzano, with some of their juices, coarsely chopped

10–12 pitted Kalamata olives, coarsely chopped

1½ tablespoons fresh flat-leaf parsley leaves

**A NOTE FROM THE BUTCHER**

Braises like this can also be prepared with lamb shanks, which make a beautiful presentation, especially when the bone is frenched. But our favorite choice for braising is the neck, which is the most flavorful and unctuously delicious cut on the lamb, in our opinion.

—Joshua Applestone, Fleisher's Grass-fed & Organic Meats, Kingston, NY

# VEAL

# VEAL PRIMER

## VEAL AT A GLANCE

**Look for** rosy pink color; moist surface; perfectly white fat; fresh smell.

**Avoid** very pale—almost white—meat (which will be bland); any off smell.

**Cuts to remember** breast, ground meat from leg, sirloin.

**Best value** breast, shank, shoulder chop.

**Splurge cuts** rack.

**Storage** 2 to 5 days in the refrigerator; 3 to 6 months in the freezer.

## BEST FLAVORS FOR VEAL

**American flavors** bacon, lemon, onions, cream.

**French flavors** Dijon mustard, cornichons, capers, rosemary, bay leaves, thyme, garlic, leeks.

**Italian flavors** sage, oregano, garlic, pancetta, porcini mushrooms, tomatoes.

Fans of veal praise its light, mild flavor, leanness, and delicate texture. Although veal is sometimes referred to as "white" meat, most of today's high-quality veal is decidedly pink. Veal is considered a luxury, especially in Europe, where it enjoys the most popularity. In Italy, veal scaloppini, veal saltimbocca, veal Milanese, and osso buco are among the country's classic dishes. French cooks prepare a variety of cuts, from tender scallops sautéed with wine and butter to bone-in breasts roasted for an elegant supper. The Germans have their own version of scaloppini, Wiener schnitzel, for which veal is pounded and breaded and then fried until golden and crispy.

**WHAT IS VEAL?** Veal is defined as a male calf of a dairy herd that is no more than 18 weeks old and weighing 450 pounds (227 kg) at the time of slaughter. The U.S. Department of Agriculture inspects all veal, although grading the meat is optional. When it is graded, more than 90 percent is deemed prime or choice, with most of the prime meat set aside for supplying restaurants. Branded veal with names such as Provimi and Dutch Valley is not graded but is usually very high quality. When you learn which brands to trust, you don't need to rely exclusively on the grading system. You can also ask your butcher questions about where the veal was sourced and how it was raised.

**ETHICAL VEAL** Perhaps because of the way it is raised, veal has never gained the same following in the United States that it has in other countries. Traditionally, most young calves were confined in extremely restrictive quarters to inhibit muscle development and were fed milk or formula to keep the meat light in color. This cruel method produced meat with all the desirable qualities—extreme leanness and tenderness, and a light color. Today, however, this "crate system" is strongly discouraged in the United States. In response to market demand, some producers turned to raising free-range veal from calves that graze on grass—or sometimes they are both bottle-fed milk and grass fed—and are permitted to roam. Veal raised in this way is redder and chewier than the meat from calves raised in limited quarters.

**VEAL AND NUTRITION** Veal is unique among meats in its nutritional profile. Because of the way calves are raised and their age at slaughter, veal never develops the kind of intramuscular fat or exterior fat that characterizes beef, pork, and lamb. Certain veal cuts, such as lean cutlets, are especially healthful in their low amount of saturated fat.

## VEAL BASICS

**TRIMMING** The guidelines for veal are the same as those for beef, but because the meat carries far less marbling, it's even more important that you leave at least ¼ inch (6 mm) of the fat intact. This will help keep the meat juicy as it cooks.

**BRINGING TO ROOM TEMPERATURE** The cooking times in this book are based on room-temperature meat. The length of time required depends on the cut and can range from 10 minutes for cutlets to 1 to 1½ hours for chops, shanks, and roasts. Always rely on your meat thermometer, not your timer, to inform you of when the meat is done. For large cuts, you can use a probe thermometer to test the temperature at the center of the meat. When the temperature reaches about 55°F (13°C), the veal is ready to cook.

**SEASONING** Because veal has a far more delicate flavor than beef, a light approach—using only salt, pepper, and mild herbs—is best for simple preparations such as panfrying chops. Similarly, marinades for veal should avoid strong flavors that might overwhelm the meat. Cutlets, or scaloppine, are sometimes coated in flour and egg, and then in herbed bread crumbs before being quickly fried. More substantial cuts are roasted with aromatics and other seasonings, or can be braised in a liquid enhanced with spices and herbs. Like other chops, veal chops can be stuffed.

**RESTING** Allowing cooked veal to rest is crucial to ensuring juicy meat that reaches its ideal level of doneness. Chops should rest for about 5 minutes; roasts need 20 to 30 minutes. Cooking forces the juices from the center of the meat toward the exterior. If you cut into the meat as soon as it is removed from the heat, many of the juices will run out. Resting allows the juices to redistribute evenly. During this time, the internal temperature of the meat rises a few degrees, allowing it to finish cooking.

**STORING** Most cuts should be consumed within 3 to 5 days. Ground veal should be cooked sooner, within up to 2 days. If you plan to freeze veal, double-wrap it securely, first with plastic wrap and then with aluminum foil, making sure that you seal the seams well. Frozen veal will keep for 4 to 6 months. Frozen ground veal is best used within 3 months. The safest way to thaw frozen meat is in the refrigerator. A 3-pound (1.5-kg) roast might require a day or longer; chops need only about 12 hours. As for other types of meats, frozen veal should not be thawed in a microwave, as the exterior will thaw but the center will remain solid, potentially encouraging the development of bacteria.

## FAQS FOR THE BUTCHER

Q: I like veal, but I have heard horror stories about how it is raised. How can I be sure that the veal I buy has been raised humanely?

A: Unlike most meat, humanely raised veal is easy to spot: just look for the "Certified Humane" label. It ensures that the meat has not been raised in unhealthy and cruel conditions. Also, ask your butcher about the veal. The best veal is generally from dairy cows that have been bred with beef bulls and allowed to nurse on their mother's milk.

Q: What is the best cut of veal for cutlets?

A: While many people make cutlets from the loin, I prefer the less expensive and more flavorful top round cut off from the leg. Since you're going to be pounding the meat anyway—and thus tenderizing it—there's no reason to waste perfectly good veal loin.

Q: What are the unsung cuts of veal?

A: For grilling, I like sirloin and marinated hearts. For braising, few things are more divine than veal shank and rolled breast. The breast is also great grilled.

—Tom Mylan, The Meat Hook, Brooklyn, NY

## COOKING BY THE CUT

**Best for panfrying** cutlets, scallops (scaloppine), tender cuts from rib and loin such as loin, rib, and top loin chops.

**Best for grilling** rib and loin chops.

**Best for roasting** rack of veal, leg, breast.

**Best for braising** shank, breast, shoulder roasts and chops, cubed shoulder.

## TAKE THE TEMPERATURE

Veal is not served rare and, with some exceptions, is seldom cooked to an internal temperature above 150° (65°C), at which point the meat becomes dry and toughens.

**Cutlets and scallops** too thin to measure the temperature; should feel just firm to the touch.

**Chops** remove from heat at 130°F (54°C); ideal temperature after resting: 135°–140°F (57°–60°C).

**Large roasts** remove from heat at 125°–130°F (52°–54°C); ideal temperature after resting: 145°F (63°C).

**Breast and shank** braised until meat falls off the bone, at 155°–165°F (68°–74°C).

## THE CUTS

The young age of veal and the smaller size of the cuts mean that the animal is broken down somewhat differently from its older counterpart, beef. Listed below and shown at right are the primary cuts, with further explanation on the characteristics and best uses for the secondary cuts.

**SHOULDER** Shoulder chops, also known as blade steaks, are best braised, to break down the collagen (connective tissue), but are also tasty when grilled just to medium-rare. Cubed shoulder meat is the ideal choice for stew. Veal shoulder achieves tenderness far more quickly than similar cuts of beef, pork, or lamb, and the collagen lends a silky texture to the braising liquid.

**RIB** The ultimate luxury cut, rib chops carry generous exterior and interior fat and yield tender and tasty meat, enhanced by its proximity to the bone. Chops may be grilled or pan roasted, and are often served with a sauce. For a special occasion, you can ask your butcher for a whole rib section—a standing rib roast of veal.

**LOIN** Resembling a T-bone steak, loin chops have a piece of tenderloin on one side of the bone and the loin on the other side. The relative lack of fat can cause loin chops to dry out more quickly than rib chops if overcooked. One way to prevent loin cuts from drying out is to incorporate fat by barding, or wrapping, fatty cuts like salt pork or bacon around the meat to baste it and keep it moist during cooking.

**LEG** Like the loin, meat from the leg section is quite lean; it requires close attention to avoid overcooking and drying out. Thin slices of leg meat from the top roast, called scallops, or scaloppine, are widely available and easy to prepare.

**BREAST** The breast, the only veal cut that carries much marbling, is an excellent candidate for roasting, slow-roasting, and braising. Breast meat can also be cubed and used in stews or it can be ground.

**FRONT LEG** Chops from the front leg can be grilled or braised. Shanks benefit from the central bone (and marrow), which keeps the meat juicy, and are best when braised.

# VEAL CHART

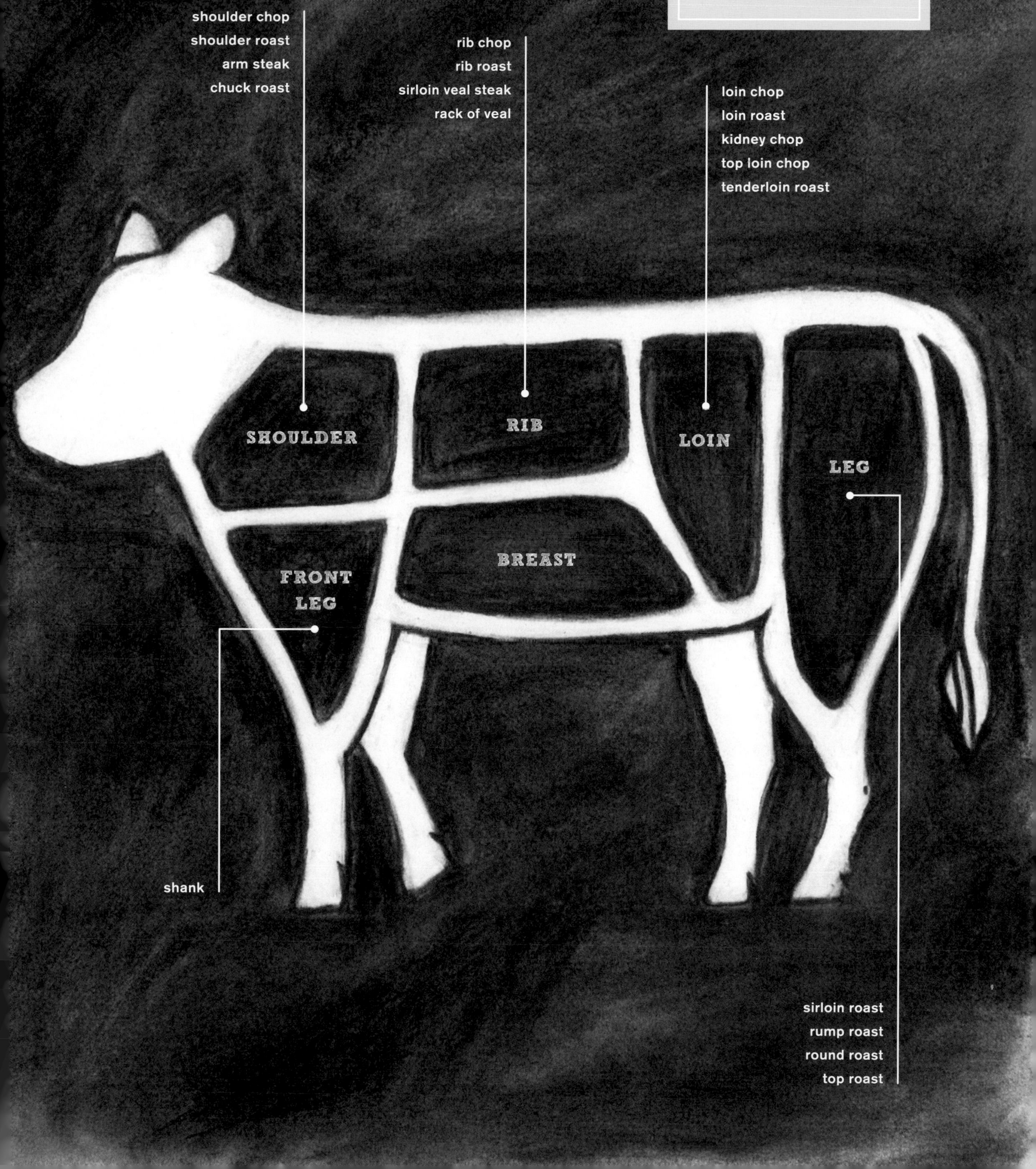
shoulder chop
shoulder roast
arm steak
chuck roast
rib chop
rib roast
sirloin veal steak
rack of veal
loin chop
loin roast
kidney chop
top loin chop
tenderloin roast
SHOULDER
RIB
LOIN
LEG
BREAST
FRONT LEG
shank
sirloin roast
rump roast
round roast
top roast

This is the quintessential summertime dinner. The veal is light and pairs perfectly with the bright flavors of the summer vegetables. With meat preparations, I always include a touch of acidity—here, from white wine and white wine vinegar—to wake up the taste buds.

Place a large, heavy frying pan over high heat and add the oil. Season both sides of the cutlets generously with salt and pepper and dust lightly on both sides with flour. When the oil is shimmering, add the cutlets and cook, without moving them, until the juices start to run from the top, about 1½ minutes. Turn and cook until firm to the touch, 1–1½ minutes more. Transfer to a plate.

Tip the pan and quickly spoon off some of the oil. Place the pan over medium heat, add the tomatoes and corn, and cook, stirring occasionally, until slightly softened, about 2 minutes. Add the vinegar and wine and simmer until almost completely reduced, 2–3 minutes. Add the broth and simmer until just slightly thickened, 1–2 minutes more. Remove the pan from the heat and add the tarragon and butter. Shake and swirl the pan vigorously until the butter melts and thickens the pan juices slightly. Taste and adjust the seasoning.

Return the cutlets to the pan and spoon some of the vegetables and sauce over the cutlets. Serve at once.

2 tablespoons olive oil

4 veal cutlets, each about ¼ inch (6 mm) thick, patted dry

Kosher salt and freshly ground pepper

Superfine flour or rice flour, in a shaker

15 cherry tomatoes, halved

1 cup (6 oz/185 g) corn kernels (from about 2 small ears)

3 tablespoons white wine vinegar

¼ cup (2 fl oz/60 ml) dry white wine

¼ cup (2 fl oz/60 ml) reduced-sodium chicken broth

1 tablespoon fresh tarragon leaves

3 tablespoons salted butter, cut into 3 pieces

---

**A NOTE FROM THE BUTCHER**

Ask if your butcher can sell you veal cutlets from the top round instead of the loin. Top round will be more tender. A good butcher will know to cut the top round across the grain.

—James Cross, Marczyk Fine Foods, Denver, CO

---

## VEAL CHOPS STUFFED WITH HERBS AND LEMON

 MAKES 2 SERVINGS

Veal rib chops carry quite a bit of fat along the bone, and if I were not stuffing them, I might be tempted to ask my butcher to french the bones. But here that extra surface area is needed to accommodate the herb and lemon stuffing. You can trim away the fat from the bones before serving, if desired. I like to accompany the chops with wilted baby spinach tossed with toasted pine nuts and dried currants.

2 veal rib chops, each about 10 oz (315 g) and 1 inch (2.5 cm) thick, patted dry

3 tablespoons minced fresh dill

2 tablespoons minced fresh oregano

1 tablespoon minced fresh sage

Grated zest of 1 small lemon

Kosher salt and freshly ground pepper

4 teaspoons plus 2 tablespoons olive oil

All-purpose flour for dredging

2 tablespoons unsalted butter

Lemon wedges for serving

Place the chops on a baking sheet and freeze, uncovered, for 20 minutes.

Working from the side of each chop away from the bone, make a horizontal cut toward the bone to form a pocket. In a bowl, stir together the dill, oregano, sage, and lemon zest. Add ¼ teaspoon salt and the 4 teaspoons oil, and stir to combine. Stuff the chops with the herb mixture. Secure the edges with 2 or 3 toothpicks, inserted diagonally. Season both sides generously with salt and pepper.

Place some flour on a plate near the stove. Place a large, heavy frying pan over medium-high heat. When it is very hot, add the 2 tablespoons oil. When the oil begins to shimmer, add the butter. As soon as the butter foam has subsided, quickly dredge the chops in the flour, shaking off the excess, and place the chops in the pan without letting them touch. Sear without moving them for 2½ minutes. Reduce the heat to medium, turn the chops, and sear for 2 minutes more. Holding the chops with tongs, sear each edge until no longer pink, 20–30 seconds. Reduce the heat to low and cook until the chops are firm to the touch and an instant-read thermometer inserted into a chop, away from the bone and not in the stuffing, registers 130°F (54°C), 1–2 minutes. Transfer to plates.

Remove the toothpicks and serve at once with the lemon wedges.

### A NOTE FROM THE BUTCHER

Other tasty cuts to look out for when hunting for a good chop for frying: pork porterhouse, pork shoulder chops, and vittellone chops. An alternative to frying the meat on top of the stove is to get your pan smoking hot, sear the meat on one side, and then flip it over and finish it in a 400°F (200°C) oven.

—Melanie Eisemann, Avedano's Holly Park Market, San Francisco, CA

I add pancetta to this classic Italian dish to heighten the natural flavors of the veal. The keys to achieving a crisp, not soggy, crust on the cutlets: use plenty of fat for frying, don't dredge the cutlets until the fat is hot, and you are ready to cook them, and never crowd the pan with too many pieces of meat.

# VEAL SCALOPPINE WITH PANCETTA AND SAGE

 MAKES 2 SERVINGS

2 veal cutlets, 4–5 oz (125–155 g) each

1 large egg

All-purpose flour for dredging

1 cup (4 oz/125 g) seasoned dried bread crumbs

4 tablespoons (2 oz/60 g) unsalted butter

3 tablespoons olive oil

2 thin pancetta slices, finely chopped

2 teaspoons minced fresh sage

⅓ cup (3 fl oz/80 ml) dry white wine

⅓ cup (3 fl oz/80 ml) reduced-sodium chicken broth

Lemon wedges for serving (optional)

Lay a large sheet of plastic wrap on a work surface, place a cutlet in the center, and cover with another sheet of plastic wrap. Use the flat side of a meat mallet to pound lightly from the center outward, gently easing the veal out to a large, even thickness of about ⅓ inch (9 mm). Repeat with the remaining cutlet. (The cutlets may be prepared up to 4 hours in advance. Refrigerate them, sandwiched between the plastic, on a baking sheet, until 10 minutes before you are ready to cook.)

In a large, shallow bowl, beat the egg lightly. Place the flour and bread crumbs in separate shallow bowls, and set the bowls near the stove.

Pat the cutlets dry. Place a 12-inch (30-cm) frying pan or sauté pan over medium-high heat and heat 3 tablespoons of the butter and the oil until sizzling. Quickly dredge both sides of the cutlets in the flour, shaking off the excess, and then dip both sides in the beaten egg. Finally, dredge in the bread crumbs, making sure both sides are coated evenly; gently shake off the excess. Place the cutlets in the pan without letting them touch. Cook without moving them until golden brown, about 1½ minutes. Turn and cook until golden and firm to the touch, about 1½ minutes more. Transfer to paper towels and turn gently to blot away the excess oil. Transfer to plates.

Pour off most of the oil from the pan, and add the pancetta and sage. Cook, stirring, until the pancetta is lightly golden, 3–4 minutes. Add the wine and broth and simmer briskly until reduced by about half. Remove the pan from the heat and add the remaining 1 tablespoon butter. Swirl the pan just until the butter has melted.

Spoon the sauce over the cutlets and serve at once with the lemon wedges.

---

**A NOTE FROM THE BUTCHER**

You could purchase a piece of veal top round and cut your own cutlets or scallops. When trimming the meat, cut off the membrane and the fat from the top and bottom, then cut across the grain to make cutlets that are about ⅓–½ inch (9–12 mm) thick. Use a meat mallet to pound the meat to the size and thickness you prefer.

—Jim Cascone, Huntington Meats, Los Angeles, CA

---

## PANFRIED VEAL CUTLETS WITH ASPARAGUS AND LEEKS

 MAKES 2 OR 3 SERVINGS

This is one of those *à la minute* dishes that is beautiful in its simplicity. The pairing of asparagus and leeks is quintessentially springlike. I like to make this dish at the start of spring when I can find tender, thin asparagus and young leeks. Make sure to prepare and measure all the ingredients before you start cooking so that you can work fast during the last few minutes of finishing the recipe.

12 thick or 24 thin asparagus spears

All-purpose flour for dredging

2 tablespoons olive oil

2–4 veal cutlets, ¾ lb (375 g) total weight, each about ¼ inch (6 mm) thick, patted dry

Kosher salt and freshly ground pepper

1 leek, white part only, finely chopped

⅓ cup (3 fl oz/80 ml) dry white wine

1 small plum tomato, seeded and cut into ¼-inch (6-mm) dice

4 fresh basil leaves, cut into narrow strips

3 tablespoons cold unsalted butter, cut into 6 pieces

Bring a large frying pan of lightly salted water to a boil. Add the asparagus and simmer until crisp tender, about 2 minutes. Drain and refresh under cold running water. Drain on a towel, cut off the tips, and set aside. Reserve the asparagus stalks for another use, such as a salad.

Place some flour in a shallow bowl near the stove. Place a large, heavy frying pan or sauté pan over medium-high heat and add the oil. Season both sides of the cutlets lightly with salt and pepper. Dredge both sides in the flour, shaking off the excess. When the oil is shimmering, add the cutlets without letting them touch. Cook without moving until the juices start to run from the top, about 1½ minutes. Turn the cutlets, push them to the side of the pan, and stir in the leek. Cook for 1 minute, reduce the heat to medium-low, and add the wine and asparagus tips. Swirl the pan to distribute the ingredients, and simmer until the asparagus is tender and most, but not all, of the liquid has been absorbed, about 2 minutes.

Stir in ¼ teaspoon salt, season with pepper, and remove the pan from the heat. Add the tomato, basil, and cold butter. Swirl the pan until the butter melts and thickens the pan juices slightly. Serve at once.

**A NOTE FROM THE BUTCHER**

Veal cutlets or scaloppine can be made from skinned and pounded veal leg meat or tenderloin. The leg is more affordable, but the cuts from the tenderloin will be so tender that all you'll need is a fork to cut through the meat.

—Harvey Gussman, Harvey's Guss Meat Co., Los Angeles, CA

To keep meat dishes healthful, I rarely use a lot of cream and butter in the same dish. But this is one of those special-occasion dishes that would be incomplete without them. Although the sauce is rich, the whole-grain mustard, capers, and cornichons add a welcome bite to a luxurious cut of veal.

Rub both sides of the chops with oil and let stand at room temperature for 1 hour.

Place a large frying pan or sauté pan over medium-high heat, and heat until very hot, about 3 minutes. Sprinkle one side of each chop generously with salt and pepper. Add the 2 teaspoons oil and the butter to the pan. As soon as the butter foams, place the chops in the pan, seasoned side down, without letting them touch. Cook without moving them for 2 minutes. Season with salt and pepper, turn, reduce the heat to medium, and cook for 2 minutes more. Transfer the chops to a platter.

Add the shallot to the pan and cook over medium heat, stirring, until softened slightly, about 1 minute. Add the wine and deglaze the pan, stirring to scrape up the browned bits from the pan bottom. Simmer until the wine has reduced to about 2 tablespoons, about 2 minutes. Stir in the cream, capers, and cornichons. Add ¼ teaspoon salt and season with pepper. Bring to a simmer, increasing the heat if necessary, and return the chops to the pan. Simmer, stirring frequently and spooning the sauce over the chops, until the sauce thickens enough to coat the back of a spoon and the chops are firm to the touch, 2–4 minutes.

Remove from the heat and immediately whisk in the mustard, whisking just until smooth. Serve at once.

## PANFRIED VEAL CHOPS WITH MUSTARD AND CORNICHON PAN SAUCE

 **MAKES 4 SERVINGS**

4 veal loin chops, each about ½ lb (250 g) and ¾ inch (2 cm) thick, patted dry

2 teaspoons olive oil, plus more for coating

Kosher salt and freshly ground pepper

2 teaspoons unsalted butter

1 large shallot, finely chopped

½ cup (4 fl oz/125 ml) dry white wine

1 cup (8 fl oz/250 ml) heavy cream

2 tablespoons capers, rinsed

5 cornichons, coarsely chopped

3 tablespoons whole-grain mustard

---

### A NOTE FROM THE BUTCHER

Veal loin chops are like the T-bone and porterhouse of veal—they have just enough fat to make them delicious. You can substitute rib chops—they are generally more expensive and are what you see at most restaurants—or veal shoulder chops, the most economical choice of the three cuts.

—Tanya Cauthen, Belmont Butchery, Richmond, VA

---

### BEEF CARPACCIO

For carpaccio, a popular Italian preparation using raw beef, best-quality tenderloin is pounded until very thin. It is topped with shavings of Parmigiano-Reggiano cheese, shaved truffles or truffle oil (optional), and baby arugula. The dish is finished with a drizzle of the very best extra-virgin olive oil and a sprinkle of flaky sea salt.

### PAILLARD

This French version of scaloppine is commonly made from veal, beef, or chicken. The meat is pounded thin and then sautéed or grilled. The thin, tender scallops are delicious drizzled with an herbed oil and served alongside a fresh green salad.

### POUNDING BONELESS CUTS

The amount of pounding required depends on the thickness of the purchased meat. To pound the meat, place on the work surface between two sheets of plastic wrap. Starting in the center and working outward, pound lightly with the flat side of a meat mallet, easing the meat into an even thickness, as specified in the recipe.

Veal Milanese (right) and Veal Scaloppine with Pancetta and Sage (page 197) both call for pounded meat, but Veal Milanese calls for pounding bone-in veal chops rather than veal scallops. The chops are pounded to a thickness of ¼ inch (6 mm), then they are breaded and sautéed to create a crispy, golden crust. The benefit of pounding bone-in chops is that the meat will cook more evenly, rather than remain rarer toward the bone.

**POUNDING BONE-IN CHOPS** Trim off most, but not all, of the surface fat from the rounded side of each chop. Sandwich each chop between two pieces of plastic wrap. With the flat side of a meat mallet, pound the meat gently, working outward, away from the bone—and being careful not to pound on the bone. Pound the meat until it is an even thickness of about ¼ inch (6 mm). Pat both sides thoroughly dry with paper towels. This step may be done up to 2 hours ahead. Refrigerate the chops, covered, until 10 minutes before cooking. Before breading the chops, season both sides generously with salt and pepper.

**BREADING THE CHOPS** Place a clean piece of plastic wrap on a work surface. Spread the bread crumbs and grated cheese on separate plates. Place the beaten eggs in a wide, shallow bowl. Dredge a chop first in the cheese, shaking off the excess. Dip in the eggs, making sure the chop is well coated on both sides, then let the excess drip back into the bowl. Place the chop in the bread crumbs, press down to coat the chop with the crumbs, turn, and press again. Set the breaded chop aside on the plastic wrap. Repeat to coat the remaining chop. Place a piece of plastic wrap on top of the breaded chops and press down firmly so that the bread crumbs adhere well. Gently remove the plastic wrap.

**COOKING TIPS** To achieve the best results when cooking the chops or other breaded meat, make sure that the butter-oil mixture or other cooking medium is hot before dredging the meat. If the chops are dredged too soon, the coating will be soggy and gummy. To test the temperature of the butter-oil mixture, add a large pinch of the bread crumbs to the pan. If the butter-oil mixture is hot enough, the crumbs will sizzle gently. Cook the chops or other meat in a large frying pan and arrange them in a single layer. When cooking many pieces of meat, use 2 large frying pans to avoid crowding.

## VEAL MILANESE

MAKES 2 SERVINGS

2 bone-in veal rib chops, each 7–8 oz (220–250 g) and ¾–1 inch (2–2.5 cm) thick

Kosher salt and freshly ground pepper

⅔ cup (1 oz/30 g) panko bread crumbs

⅔ cup (2½ oz/75 g) finely grated Parmigiano-Reggiano cheese

1 large egg plus 2 large yolks

¼ cup (2 fl oz/60 ml) olive oil

4 tablespoons (2 oz/60 g) butter

1 tablespoon finely chopped fresh flat-leaf parsley

Lemon wedges for serving

Line a baking sheet with paper towels and place in a very low oven to warm.

Season the chops on both sides with salt and pepper. Spread the bread crumbs and grated cheese on separate plates. Whisk the eggs in a wide, shallow bowl.

Place a 12-inch (30-cm) frying pan over medium heat. When it is hot, add the oil and butter. Working quickly, bread the chops as directed at left.

Add the chops to the pan without letting them touch. Cook without moving them until they are golden brown and crusty, about 4 minutes. Every 30 seconds, spoon some hot fat over the bones. Turn the chops and cook until golden, 3–4 minutes more, continuing to baste the bones. Transfer to the baking sheet in the oven and let rest for 2–3 minutes.

Place on plates, garnish with the parsley, and serve with lemon wedges.

### BUTTER DRIZZLE

A traditional pan sauce would render your hard-won and perfectly crisp coating soggy, but try a drizzle of sizzling butter: While the chops are resting, drain off and discard the cooking fat from the pan and quickly wipe with a paper towel. Return the pan to low heat, add 2 tablespoons butter, and swirl the pan until it melts and sizzles. Drizzle each chop with a little butter and serve at once.

MAKES 6–8 SERVINGS

Veal breast is a popular, low-cost cut in the Italian kitchen. The meat is somewhat fatty, but that is part of its appeal. I love stuffing this cut with a good melting cheese such as fontina; it oozes out when the meat is sliced open. The Madeira-soaked porcini meld with the meat juices to create an earthy sauce for drizzling. Be careful to watch the braising and provide enough liquid so that the meat doesn't scorch.

In a heatproof measuring cup, combine the porcini with ¾ cup (6 fl oz/ 180 ml) hot water. Add the Madeira and let stand for 20 minutes. Strain well, reserving the soaking liquid. Squeeze the mushrooms as dry as possible, then chop coarsely. Set aside.

Place the veal breast, fat side down, on a work surface. Season generously with salt and pepper. Lay the fontina slices lengthwise across the center, leaving 1 inch (2.5 cm) uncovered at each end. Scatter the porcini, garlic, and thyme over the cheese. Starting at a long side, roll the meat up tightly into a cylinder. Tie firmly every 2 inches (5 cm) with kitchen string. Tie lengthwise with a long piece of string, to help seal the cheese inside. Pat the meat thoroughly dry and season lightly with salt and pepper.

Place a Dutch oven or other large, heavy pot over medium heat, and add the oil and butter. When the butter foam has subsided, add the roll and cook until golden on all sides, about 2½ minutes on each of 3 or 4 sides. Add the wine and ¼ cup (2 fl oz/60 ml) of the reserved mushroom-soaking liquid. Adjust the heat so that the liquid simmers very gently—a few occasional bubbles, not more.

Partially cover the pot and braise for 1¾–2 hours, turning the roll every 15–20 minutes. If you have trouble maintaining the low heat, use a heat diffuser. Turn the roll and check the liquid level occasionally; adjust the heat as necessary and add 1 tablespoon mushroom-soaking liquid if necessary. The meat is done when it is very tender and an instant-read thermometer inserted into the center of the meat registers about 155°F (68°C).

Transfer to a platter and let rest, loosely covered with aluminum foil, for 10 minutes. Add 2 tablespoons mushroom-soaking liquid to the pot and simmer over medium heat until reduced slightly, 3–4 minutes. Snip the strings and cut the roll into thick slices. Drizzle with the pan juices and serve at once.

About ⅓ cup (⅓ oz/10 g) dried porcini mushrooms

2 tablespoons Madeira or medium-dry sherry

1 boneless center-cut veal breast, about 3 lb (1 kg)

Kosher salt and freshly ground pepper

2 oz (60 g) Italian fontina cheese, cut into slices ¼ inch (6 mm) thick

5 cloves garlic, minced

2 teaspoons chopped fresh thyme

1 tablespoon olive oil

2 tablespoons unsalted butter

¼ cup (2 fl oz/60 ml) dry white wine

**A NOTE FROM THE BUTCHER**

This cut can be hard to find. It is a long, flat, bony piece of meat that looks like a pork sparerib, only bigger. The true breast is only half the piece, with the other side being the brisket, which is usually boned for stew or ground veal. A boneless piece of veal shoulder, butterflied flat, is a good substitute.

—Don Kuzaro, Jr., Don & Joe's Meats, Seattle, WA

# VEAL STEW WITH ROSEMARY AND LEMONY GREENS

 MAKES 6 SERVINGS

This tangy, summery stew is an updated variation of an old-fashioned French dish called *blanquette de veau*. In my version, the white sauce (the blanket) is thinner, making it just the right consistency for spooning over orzo or rice, and has two acidic notes, lemon juice and wine. You can substitute other greens for the kale, such as beet greens, or even spinach, adjusting the cooking time so that the vegetables retain their color.

2 large fresh rosemary sprigs

2 fresh flat-leaf parsley sprigs

2 bay leaves

2 lb (1 kg) veal shoulder, cut into 2-inch (5-cm) cubes, rinsed under cool water

2 ribs celery, finely diced

2 leeks, white part only, finely chopped

1½ tablespoons fresh lemon juice, plus more if needed

1¼ cups (10 fl oz/310 ml) dry white wine

1¾ cups (14 fl oz/430 ml) reduced-sodium chicken broth or homemade chicken or vegetable stock

Pinch of ground nutmeg

Kosher salt and freshly ground pepper

1 tablespoon unsalted butter, at room temperature

1 tablespoon all-purpose flour

½ cup (4 oz/125 g) crème fraîche or sour cream

2 large egg yolks

## FOR THE LEMONY GREENS

3 tablespoons olive oil

3 cloves garlic, minced

1 lb (500 g) young kale, stems removed

1 lemon, halved

Kosher salt and freshly ground pepper

Tie the rosemary, parsley, and bay leaves together with kitchen string. In a Dutch oven or other large, heavy pot, combine the tied herbs, veal, celery, leeks, the 1½ tablespoons lemon juice, wine, broth, and nutmeg. Add 1½ teaspoons salt and season with pepper. Add 1 cup (8 fl oz/250 ml) water. The liquid should barely cover the ingredients; add water if necessary.

Place over high heat and bring just to a boil. Immediately reduce the heat so that the liquid simmers very gently. Cook, partially covered, until the meat is tender, 1–1¼ hours, occasionally skimming off any scum that rises to the surface.

In a small bowl, blend the butter and flour together into a paste. With a slotted spoon, transfer the veal and some of the vegetables to a platter. Tent loosely with aluminum foil. Strain the braising liquid into a clean saucepan, discarding the solids. Whisk the butter-flour paste into the liquid. Bring to a simmer over medium-high heat and simmer briskly, whisking occasionally, until reduced slightly, about 10 minutes.

Meanwhile, prepare the lemony greens: Place a large frying pan over medium-high heat and add the oil. Add the garlic and cook, stirring, for 10 seconds. Add the kale, reduce the heat to medium-low, cover, and cook, stirring frequently, until the kale is wilted but not falling apart, about 5 minutes. Remove from the heat and squeeze the lemon halves over the kale. Season with salt and pepper.

In a bowl, whisk together the crème fraîche, if using, the egg yolks, and ½ cup (4 fl oz/125 ml) of the warm braising liquid; set aside. Return the veal to the braising liquid and adjust the heat so that the liquid barely simmers. Warm the veal through for 3–5 minutes. Taste and adjust the seasoning with salt, pepper, and lemon juice. Stir in the egg yolk mixture and warm until the liquid is just on the verge of simmering, 1–2 minutes; do not allow it to boil, or the yolks will curdle. The liquid will thicken to a light coating consistency. If using sour cream, stir it into the stew.

Ladle the stew into bowls, top with the greens, and serve at once.

Veal shoulder chops, also known as veal blade steaks, are far less expensive than rib or loin chops, yet are still tender enough to be cooked with a dry-heat method such as grilling, as long as you are careful not to overcook them. I suggest accompanying them with a rich sauce or topping, as in the aioli here. One chop can be sliced off the bone to serve two or even three people, depending on the size.

In a resealable plastic bag, combine the oil, lemon juice, thyme, rosemary, and garlic. Add ½ teaspoon salt and season with black pepper. Add the veal chops, squeeze most of the air from of the bag, and massage the bag to distribute the ingredients evenly. Refrigerate for at least 1 hour or up to 4 hours. Remove from the refrigerator and let stand at room temperature for 1 hour before grilling.

To make the aioli, bring a small saucepan of water to a boil. Add the tarragon and blanch for 30 seconds. Drain, rinse with cold water, and pat dry. In a food processor, combine the tarragon, garlic, egg, vinegar, mustard, and ¾ teaspoon salt. Pulse to blend. With the motor running, drizzle in the olive and canola oils very slowly at first, then add at a slightly faster rate after the first ⅓ cup (3 fl oz/80 ml) oil has been emulsified. Add the lemon juice and white pepper and pulse two or three times. Cover and refrigerate until serving.

Prepare a charcoal or gas grill for direct-heat grilling over medium-high heat, or preheat a cast-iron stove-top grill pan over high heat. Remove the chops from the marinade, and pat thoroughly dry; discard the marinade. Season both sides of the chops with salt and black pepper. Place the chops on the grill rack over the hottest part of the fire or in the grill pan, and cook for 2½ minutes. Move the chops after 1 minute if the coals flame or the chops are in danger of charring. Turn and cook for 2½ minutes more. Move the chops to a cooler part of the grill or reduce the heat, and continue to cook until firm to the touch, about 2 minutes per side. Transfer to a cutting board and let rest, loosely covered, for about 5 minutes.

Carve the meat away from the bones and cut the meat into thick strips. Divide among plates and serve at once with the aioli.

# GRILLED VEAL CHOPS WITH MUSTARD-TARRAGON AIOLI

 MAKES 4 SERVINGS

2 tablespoons olive oil

1 tablespoon fresh lemon juice

¼ teaspoon dried thyme or 2 fresh thyme sprigs

1 teaspoon minced fresh rosemary

1 clove garlic, minced

Kosher salt and freshly ground black pepper

2 veal shoulder chops, each about 1 lb (500 g) and ¾ inch (2 cm) thick

## FOR THE MUSTARD-TARRAGON AIOLI

About ⅓ cup (½ oz/15 g) firmly packed tarragon leaves

1 large clove garlic, chopped

1 large egg, at room temperature

2 teaspoons white wine vinegar

1 tablespoon Dijon mustard

Kosher salt

½ cup (4 fl oz/125 ml) extra-virgin olive oil

½ cup (4 fl oz/125 ml) canola oil

2 tablespoons fresh lemon juice

¼ teaspoon ground white pepper

## VEAL BOLOGNESE

MAKES 6 SERVINGS

3 tablespoons olive oil

1 small white onion, finely chopped

1 carrot, peeled and finely chopped

1 rib celery, finely chopped

1 small clove garlic, minced

2 or 3 bay leaves

5 oz (155 g) ground veal

5 oz (155 g) ground pork

5 oz (155 g) lean ground beef

1 cup (8 fl oz/250 ml) full-bodied red wine, such as Zinfandel

2 cans (28 oz/875 g each) plum tomatoes, preferably San Marzano, with their juices

1 cup (8 fl oz/250 ml) heavy cream

Kosher salt and freshly ground pepper

½ cup (2 oz/60 g) grated Parmigiano-Reggiano cheese

8 large fresh basil leaves, coarsely chopped

1½ lb (750 g) spaghetti, cooked according to the package directions, for serving

To make the sauce the authentic Italian way, squeeze each tomato as you add it to the pot, to begin the process of breaking them down into a thick, delicious sauce. Toss the just-drained pasta in the empty cooking pot with a few tablespoons of butter and about one-fourth of the sauce before mounding into pasta bowls, then top with the remaining sauce.

Place a Dutch oven or other large, heavy pot over medium-low heat and add the oil. Add the onion, carrot, and celery and cook, stirring occasionally, until the onion is translucent, about 10 minutes. Add the garlic and bay leaves and cook for 1 minute more.

Add the veal, pork, and beef, and cook, stirring to break up the chunks, until the beef is no longer pink, about 7 minutes. Add the wine, raise the heat to high, and cook for about 5 minutes to reduce the wine slightly. Add the tomatoes and their juices and the cream and reduce the heat to low. Cook, uncovered, stirring every 10 minutes or so, for about 1½ hours.

Add ¾ teaspoon salt, season with pepper, and cook for about 10 minutes more. Taste and adjust the seasoning. Stir in the cheese and basil. Serve at once over the pasta.

### A NOTE FROM THE BUTCHER

If you don't have all three meats—pork, veal, and beef—for this sauce, you could use two of the three and still make a fabulous bolognese. Or, even better, add any delicious meat that you have on hand, like bacon, sausage, or guanciale. I like to use the ends of the prosciutto, but they are very hard, so I chop them in a food processor first. Remember, if you use any kind of cured meat, you'll want to cut down on the salt.

—Joshua Applestone, Fleisher's Grass-fed & Organic Meats, Kingston, NY

## ROASTED VEAL BREAST WITH GREEN OLIVES AND THYME

 MAKES 4 OR 5 SERVINGS

Veal breast on the bone is a favorite cut in French and Italian households because it is tasty and economical and does not take forever to cook. When the cut is roasted, the meat is juicy, and the bone side becomes crisp. You can stir other seasonal ingredients into the pan sauce at the end of cooking. Dried fruits, such as cherries, prunes, or apricots are especially delicious.

1 bone-in veal breast, about 4½ lb (2.25 kg), chine bone removed

2 tablespoons olive oil

2 tablespoons coarsely chopped fresh thyme

Kosher salt and freshly ground pepper

1 white or yellow onion, thinly sliced

⅔ cup (5 fl oz/160 ml) white wine

1 teaspoon white wine vinegar

2 cups (10 oz/315 g) mild green olives, such as Picholine or Lucques, pitted and quartered

Small handful of coarsely chopped fresh herbs, such as flat-leaf parsley, dill, chives, or basil

Remove the veal from the refrigerator and let stand at room temperature for 1½ hours. Preheat the oven to 500°F (260°C) and place a rack in the upper third of the oven.

Pat the veal thoroughly dry. Brush all over with the oil. Season with the thyme and generously with salt and pepper. Mound the onion slices in a roasting pan and place the veal, bone side down, on the onion.

Place in the oven and roast for 20 minutes. Turn and roast for 10 minutes more. Reduce the oven temperature to 350°F (180°C), turn the veal bone side down again, and add ⅓ cup (3 fl oz/80 ml) of the wine and the vinegar to the pan. Cover securely with heavy-duty aluminum foil, crimping all around the edges. Roast until an instant-read thermometer inserted into the thickest and meatiest part of the veal, away from the bone, registers 155°F (68°C), about 50 minutes. Transfer the veal to a platter, tent loosely with aluminum foil, and let rest for 10–15 minutes.

Meanwhile, tip the roasting pan and spoon off some of the fat, if desired. Add the remaining wine and 2 tablespoons water to the pan and place over medium-high heat. Simmer briskly for about 5 minutes to concentrate the pan juices. Stir in the olives and herbs and remove from the heat.

Working on the top side, carve the meat from the bones into thick slices on the diagonal. Cut the bones apart. Arrange the meat and bones on plates. Top with the olives and pan juices. Serve at once.

### A NOTE FROM THE BUTCHER

Try wrapping the veal breast in *lardo*, cured pork fat sold at Italian markets and specialty-food stores. This is a way to keep any cut from getting too dry while cooking, and it lends the meat a delicate flavor. If you can't find lardo, you can use bacon as a tasty wrapper.

—William Evans, Clancey's Meats & Fish, Minneapolis, MN

# SALADS, SIDES & TOPPINGS

## MANGO SALSA

**MAKES ABOUT 2½ CUPS (18 OZ/560 G)**

2 cups (12 oz/375 g) diced mango

1 small serrano chile, seeded and minced

6 green onions, thinly sliced

¾ cup (¾ oz/20 g) coarsely chopped fresh cilantro

½ red bell pepper, seeded and finely diced

3 tablespoons fresh lime juice

Kosher salt

In a bowl, combine all the ingredients, including 1 teaspoon salt, and toss gently. Cover and refrigerate for 30 minutes before serving.

## HORSERADISH CRÈME FRAÎCHE

**MAKES 1¼ CUPS (9 OZ/220 G)**

3 tablespoons freshly grated horseradish

1 cup (8 oz/250 g) crème fraîche

1 tablespoon plus 2 teaspoons finely snipped fresh chives

½ teaspoon ground white pepper

In a bowl, whisk together all the ingredients. Cover and refrigerate for 30 minutes before serving.

## AIOLI

**MAKES 1¼ CUPS (10 FL OZ/310 ML)**

10 large cloves garlic

1 large egg, at room temperature

1 tablespoon red wine vinegar

1 teaspoon Dijon mustard

Kosher salt

¾ cup (6 fl oz/180 ml) extra-virgin olive oil

¼ cup (2 fl oz/60 ml) canola oil

1½ tablespoons fresh lemon juice

¼ teaspoon white pepper

In a saucepan, combine the garlic with water to cover, bring to a boil, and boil for 30 seconds. Drain and let the garlic cool for 5 minutes. In a food processor, combine the cooked garlic, egg, vinegar, mustard, and ½ teaspoon salt and puree until smooth. With the motor running, slowly add the oils, processing until incorporated. Add the lemon juice and white pepper and pulse to mix.

**VARIATION** For Orange-Tapenade Aioli, stir the grated zest of 1 orange and 2 tablespoons olive tapenade into the aioli.

## SUN-DRIED TOMATO JAM

**MAKES ABOUT 1 CUP (10 OZ/315 G)**

2 cups (10 oz/315 g) drained oil-packed sun-dried tomatoes, coarsely chopped

1 tablespoon extra-virgin olive oil

2 cloves garlic, minced

½ red onion, thinly sliced

1 tablespoon sugar

¼ cup (2 fl oz/60 ml) red wine vinegar

½ teaspoon dried thyme

Sea salt and freshly ground pepper

In a saucepan over medium heat, combine the tomatoes, oil, garlic, and onion and cook, stirring, until the onion begins to brown, about 5 minutes. Stir in the sugar, vinegar, and thyme. Add 1 cup (8 fl oz/250 ml) water and ½ teaspoon each salt and pepper, bring to a boil, reduce the heat to low, cover, and simmer for 30 minutes. Uncover, raise the heat to medium-high, and cook until thick, about 5 minutes.

## GARLIC CROÛTES

**MAKES 6 CROÛTES**

6 thick slices coarse country bread

1–2 tablespoons extra-virgin olive oil

Sea salt and freshly ground pepper

2 cloves garlic, halved crosswise

Preheat the oven to 350°F (180°C). Brush the bread slices on both sides with the oil, season with salt and pepper, and place on a baking sheet. Bake until golden, 10–15 minutes. Rub the top side of each slice with the cut side of a garlic clove.

## TOASTED GARLIC BREAD CRUMBS

**MAKES ABOUT 1 CUP (4 OZ/125 G)**

3 thick slices coarse country bread

3 cloves garlic

Sea salt and freshly ground pepper

2 tablespoons extra-virgin olive oil

Discard the crusts and tear the bread into chunks. In a food processor, pulse the garlic until minced. Add the bread, ½ teaspoon salt, and a pinch of pepper. Pulse into coarse crumbs. In a small nonstick frying pan over medium heat, warm the oil. Add the crumb mixture and cook, stirring, until crisp and golden brown, 2–3 minutes. Store in an airtight container in the freezer for up to 6 months.

## ONION RINGS

### MAKES 2–4 SERVINGS

1 cup (5 oz/155 g) all-purpose flour

¾ cup (6 fl oz/ 180 ml) light ale

Canola oil for deep-frying

2 large yellow onions, cut into slices ⅛–¼ inch (3–6 mm) thick

Kosher salt and freshly ground pepper

In a large bowl, stir together the flour and ale until smooth.

Pour the oil to a depth of 3 inches (7.5 cm) into a deep, heavy saucepan and heat to 365°F (185°C) on a deep-frying thermometer. Working in batches, add the onion slices to the batter and toss to coat evenly, then add to the hot oil and fry until golden brown, 1–2 minutes. Using a slotted spoon, transfer to paper towels to drain, then sprinkle with salt and pepper. Serve at once.

## HERBED COUSCOUS

### MAKES 4 SERVINGS

¾ cup (4½ oz/140 g) instant couscous

2 tablespoons capers, rinsed and chopped

2 tablespoons minced fresh dill

¼ cup (1½ oz/45 g) minced red onion

1 cup (8 fl oz/250 ml) reduced-sodium chicken broth

2 tablespoons dry white wine

1 tablespoon extra-virgin olive oil

1 tablespoon white wine vinegar

Freshly ground pepper

In a heatproof bowl, combine the couscous, capers, dill, and onion. In a small saucepan, bring the broth and wine to a simmer. Pour over the couscous. Cover the bowl with a plate and let stand for 5 minutes. Fluff with a fork and stir in the oil and vinegar. Add a generous pinch of pepper. Serve warm or at room temperature.

## CREAMY WHITE BEANS

### MAKES 2–3 SERVINGS

2 tablespoons olive oil

1 leek, white part only, finely chopped

1 clove garlic, minced

1 can (15 oz/470 g) cannellini beans, rinsed and drained

1 teaspoon fresh lemon juice

Kosher salt and freshly ground pepper

1 tablespoon heavy cream

1 tablespoon coarsely chopped fresh flat-leaf parsley

1 teaspoon minced fresh rosemary

In a frying pan over medium-low heat, warm 1 tablespoon of the oil. Add the leek and cook, stirring occasionally, until softened, about 5 minutes. Add the garlic, stir once, and remove from the heat. In a food processor, combine the beans, the remaining 1 tablespoon oil, the lemon juice, ¼ teaspoon salt, and a few grinds of pepper and process until smooth. Stir the bean mixture into the leeks and add the cream,

parsley, and rosemary. Place over medium-low heat until warmed through. Serve at once.

## ROASTED KALE STRIPS

### MAKES 4–6 SERVINGS

2 bunches kale

Extra-virgin olive oil for coating

Kosher salt

Preheat the oven to 350°F (180°C). Discard the kale stems and cut the leaves crosswise into strips about 1 inch (2.5 cm) wide. Place the kale on a rimmed baking sheet and toss with just enough oil to coat the leaves lightly. Season generously with salt. Roast for 15 minutes. Toss and continue to roast until very crispy, 7–10 minutes more. Serve hot or at warm room temperature.

## LIME, CABBAGE, AND JALAPEÑO SLAW

### MAKES 6–8 SERVINGS

¼ cup (2 fl oz/60 ml) fresh lime juice

¼ cup (2 oz/60 g) sour cream

¼ cup (2 fl oz/60 ml) mayonnaise

½ teaspoon chile powder

1 jalapeño chile, seeded and minced

1 cup (1 oz/30 g) loosely packed fresh cilantro leaves, minced

Kosher salt

1 head green cabbage, about 1½ lb (750 g), cored, tough outer leaves removed, and thinly sliced crosswise

In a large nonreactive bowl, whisk together the lime juice, sour cream, mayonnaise, chile powder, jalapeño, cilantro, and 1 teaspoon salt. Add the cabbage and toss to mix. Cover and refrigerate for 1 hour to allow the flavors to marry. Serve slightly chilled, tossing again to distribute the dressing just before serving.

### FENNEL-PARSLEY SLAW

MAKES 4 SERVINGS

Grated zest of 1 lemon

1 tablespoon plus 1 teaspoon fresh lemon juice

2 teaspoons dried oregano

Kosher salt and freshly ground pepper

2 tablespoons extra-virgin olive oil

2 tablespoons mayonnaise

2 large fennel bulbs, about 1½ lb (750 g) total weight

⅔ cup (1 oz/30 g) minced fresh flat-leaf parsley

1 red bell pepper, seeded and cut into matchsticks

In a large bowl, whisk together the lemon zest and juice and the oregano. Add ¾ teaspoon salt and season with pepper. Whisk in the oil and mayonnaise.

Trim the stalks from the fennel bulbs and discard. Quarter each bulb and trim away the triangle of core at the base. Cut the quarters crosswise as thinly as possible. Add the fennel, parsley, and bell pepper to the bowl and toss to coat all the ingredients evenly. Serve immediately, or cover and refrigerate for up to 1 hour, then toss again just before serving.

### TOMATO-BASIL SALAD

MAKES 4 SERVINGS

2 large, ripe beefsteak-style tomatoes, about 1¼ lb (625 g) total weight, halved, seeded, and cut into ¼-inch (6-mm) dice

1 teaspoon grated lemon zest

1 tablespoon fresh lemon juice

1 tablespoon balsamic vinegar

Kosher salt and freshly ground pepper

½ cup (¾ oz/20 g) coarsely chopped fresh basil

3 tablespoons extra-virgin olive oil

In a bowl, combine the tomatoes, lemon zest, lemon juice, and vinegar. Add ½ teaspoon salt, season with pepper, and toss well. Add the basil and oil and toss gently. Adjust the seasoning and serve at once.

### ENDIVE SALAD

MAKES 2–3 SERVINGS

2 small shallots, finely chopped

3 tablespoons balsamic vinegar

1 tablespoon grated orange zest

1 tablespoon fresh orange juice

¼ cup (2 fl oz/60 ml) best-quality extra-virgin olive oil

Kosher salt and freshly ground pepper

3 small or 2 large heads Belgian endive

3 cups (3 oz/90 g) mâche lettuce or baby spinach

⅓ cup (2 oz/60 g) pine nuts, toasted and coarsely chopped

1½ oz (45 g) Parmesan cheese

In a bowl, whisk together the shallots, vinegar, orange zest and juice, and oil. Whisk in ¼ teaspoon salt and season with pepper. Cover and refrigerate until serving.

Core the endive heads, then cut lengthwise into slivers. Add to the dressing and toss thoroughly. Fold in the lettuce and pine nuts. Shave the Parmesan over the top. Serve at once.

### LEMONY CAESAR SALAD

MAKES 3–6 SERVINGS

3 large cloves garlic

1 large egg yolk

3 anchovy fillets, soaked in water for 5 minutes and patted dry

3 tablespoons fresh lemon juice

1 tablespoon Dijon mustard

1 teaspoon red wine vinegar

1 teaspoon Worcestershire sauce

Kosher salt and freshly ground pepper

⅓ cup (3 fl oz/80 ml) canola or olive oil

6–8 pale inner hearts of romaine lettuce

In a mini food processor, pulse the garlic until minced. Add the egg yolk, anchovies, lemon juice, mustard, vinegar, Worcestershire sauce, ¼ teaspoon salt and several grinds of pepper and pulse until puréed. Add the oil and pulse until thoroughly emulsified. Cover and refrigerate until serving.

With a sharp knife, cut the romaine crosswise into pieces about 1½ inches (4 cm) wide. Soak for 5–10 minutes in very cold water. In batches, spin thoroughly dry, wrap in a large kitchen towel, and place in a plastic bag. Refrigerate until serving.

In a large bowl, toss the chilled romaine with the dressing. Season with pepper and serve at once.

## WEST

### 4505 MEATS

San Francisco Ferry Building Farmer's Market
San Francisco, CA 94111
(415) 255-3094
www.4505meats.com

SPECIALTY Featherlight chicharrones (cracklings) and uncured hot dogs.

FAVORITE CUT Neck (of any animal).

ABOUT Founded in 2009 by Ryan Farr and his wife, Cesalee, 4505 Meats sells its meats at the Ferry Building Farmer's Market on Thursdays from 10 am to 2 pm and Saturdays from 8 am to 2 pm. A classically trained chef, Ryan honed his butchery techniques during his restaurant kitchen days and now teaches butchery classes in the Bay Area.

### ALEXANDER'S PRIME MEATS AND CATERING

6580 N. San Gabriel Blvd.
San Gabriel, CA 91775
(626) 286 6767
www.alexandersprimemeats.com

SPECIALTY Prime beef dry-aged for a minimum of 21 days.

FAVORITE CUT Rib-eye or New York strip roast.

ABOUT This seventy-five-year-old meat purveyor is located in a full-service gourmet market. Its butchers together boast 450 years of meat-cutting experience.

### AVEDANO'S HOLLY PARK MARKET

235 Cortland Ave.
San Francisco, CA 94110
(415) 285-MEAT (6328)
www.avedanos.com

SPECIALTY Old-fashioned cuts from responsibly raised animals.

FAVORITE CUT Too hard to choose one.

ABOUT The mission of this women-owned neighborhood market is to provide customers "with great food they can feel confident eating."

### BRYAN'S FINE FOODS

341 Corte Madera Town Center
Corte Madera, CA 94925
(415) 927-4488
www.bryansfinefoods.com

SPECIALTY Prime dry-aged beef.

FAVORITE CUT Dry-aged bone-in rib steak.

ABOUT San Francisco–born Bryan Flannery has been in the meat business since he was old enough to sweep the floors in the family meat market. He remembers accompanying his father on meat-buying trips, back in the days when it was possible to hand-pick a side of beef. Today, Bryan works tirelessly to ensure that Bryan's Fine Foods, soon to be renamed Flannery Beef, carries only the finest meat available.

### DON AND JOE'S MEATS

85 Pike St.
Seattle, WA 98101
(206) 682-7670
www.donandjoesmeats.com

SPECIALTY Full line of beef, pork, lamb, veal, poultry, and hard-to-find specialty meats and cuts, such as veal sweetbreads, osso buco, and hanger steak.

FAVORITE CUT Bone-in rib steak.

ABOUT This traditional market is operated by Don Kuzaro, Jr., who began working as a "clean-up kid" in the shop in 1969, the year his father and his uncle Joe opened it.

### HARVEY'S GUSS MEAT CO.

949 S. Ogden Dr.
Los Angeles, CA 90036
(323) 937-4622
www.harveysgussmeat.com

SPECIALTY Prime Angus beef dry-aged on the premises.

FAVORITE CUT Tuscan porterhouse, 2½ to 3 inches (6 to 7.5 cm) thick.

ABOUT Harvey Gussman and his brother took over the business from their father in 1966, and Harvey remains at the helm. Primarily a wholesale operation, Harvey's Guss supplies meat to the area's top restaurants and retailers, and to consumers with one-day advance notice.

### HUNTINGTON MEATS

6333 W. Third St., Ste. 350
Los Angeles, CA 90036
(323) 938-5383
www.huntingtonmeats.com

SPECIALTY House-made sausages, Colorado lamb, Kobe beef, Kurobuta-Berkshire pork, and game.

FAVORITE CUT Cowboy-cut porterhouse steak, 2½ inches (6 cm) thick.

ABOUT Opened in 1986 in the historic Los Angeles Farmers' Market, Huntington Meats is widely regarded as one of the city's top butcher shops.

### LAURELHURST MARKET

3155 E. Burnside St.
Portland, Oregon 97214
(503) 206-3099
www.laurelhurstmarket.com

SPECIALTY Natural meats, house-made charcuterie, smoked meats, and pâtés.

FAVORITE CUT  Bavette steak.

ABOUT  In May 2009, Laurelhurst opened as a butcher shop inside a steakhouse. At lunchtime, it sells sandwiches made with its own house-made deli meats. At night, it turns into a full-scale steak house. In 2010, it was named one of the country's top ten new restaurants by *Bon Appétit* magazine.

## LINDY AND GRUNDY'S MEATS

801 North Fairfax Ave., No. 105
Los Angeles, CA 90046
(323) 951-0804
www.lindyandgrundy.com

SPECIALTY  Whole-animal butchery of locally sourced meats and house-cured, smoked, and prepared meats.

FAVORITE CUT  Hamburger (Erika) and pork butt (Amelia).

ABOUT  After apprenticing at Fleisher's Grass-Fed and Organic Meats in Kingston, New York, Erika Nakamura and Amelia Posada moved to Los Angeles and opened this custom-cut shop in January 2011.

## MARCZYK FINE FOODS

770 E. Seventeenth Ave.
Denver, CO 80203
(303) 894-9499
www.marczyk.com

SPECIALTY  Niman Ranch meats, homemade sausages.

FAVORITE CUT  Pedro steak (a tri-tip steak).

ABOUT  Opened in 2002, Marczyk Fine Foods is a full-service, family-owned urban grocery store. Owners Pete and Paul Marczyk travel the globe to find the finest items for their loyal neighborhood shoppers.

## THE MEAT SHOP

202 E. Buckeye Rd.
Phoenix, AZ 85004
(602) 258-5075
www.themeatshopaz.com

SPECIALTY  Fresh, natural pork and grass-fed beef.

FAVORITE CUT  Bacon in four styles: regular, rasher, buckboard, and guanciale.

ABOUT  In 2008, at a time when the word locavore was just entering the language, Tim and Beth Wilson opened The Meat Shop, which sells only locally raised meats, including pork raised on their family farm.

# MIDWEST

## CLANCEY'S MEATS AND FISH

4307 Upton Ave. S
Minneapolis, MN 55410
(612) 926-0222
www.clanceysmeats.com

SPECIALTY  Local meats from humanely raised animals, house-made sausages, cured and roasted meats, and award-winning sandwiches.

FAVORITE CUT  Skirt steak, hanger steak, lamb blade chop, and pork belly.

ABOUT  Clancey's, which has been in business since 2003, has worked with the same top-notch farmers since opening day.

## GEPPERTH'S MEAT MARKET

1964 N. Halsted St.
Chicago, IL 60614
(773) 549-3883
www.goforclover.com

SPECIALTY  Homemade sausages, prime meat, Angus choice beef.

FAVORITE CUT  Prime rib steak.

ABOUT  Otto Demke and his wife, Diana, bought Gepperth's in 1981 from the Gepperth brothers, whose father had founded the store in 1906. Today, it is recognized as one of the oldest continuously operating markets in the city.

## NELSON'S MEAT MARKET

1140 Old Marion Rd. NE
Cedar Rapids, IA 52402
(319) 393-8161
www.nelsonsmeat.com

SPECIALTY  Angus beef and locally grown pork.

FAVORITE CUT  "Miami roll" (Nelson's unique creation: pork tenderloins wrapped in flank steak and then wrapped in bacon).

ABOUT  Weir Nelson opened Nelson's in 1935. His son joined him in the early 1950s, and current owner Mark Martin became a partner in 1969, then took over from the younger Weir in 1995. Nelson's continues to offer the personalized service and high-quality meats that distinguished its early days.

## ZIER'S PRIME MEATS AND POULTRY

813 Ridge Rd.
Wilmette, IL 60091
(847) 251-4000
www.ziersprime.com

SPECIALTY  Prime beef, natural pork and poultry, game, and small-batch sausages.

ABOUT  Twenty-five years ago, Dave Zier and his wife, Denise, transformed an aging neighborhood market in operation since the 1890s into this premium butcher shop.

# EAST

## BELMONT BUTCHERY

15 N. Belmont Ave.
Richmond, VA 23221
(804) 422-8519
www.belmontbutchery.com

SPECIALTY Hand-cut local grass-fed and pasture-raised beef and handmade sausages.

FAVORITE CUT Everything, from a thick steak to a thin slice of dry-aged beef.

ABOUT Opened in October 2006 by Swiss-trained chef turned butcher Tanya Cauthen, Belmont Butchery features meats from local farms hand-cut to order. The shop's motto reveals the butchers' no-nonsense approach: If we don't have it, we will get it. If we can't get it, you probably don't really need it!

## FLEISHER'S GRASS-FED & ORGANIC MEATS

307 Wall St.
Kingston, NY 12401
(845) 338-MOOO (6666)
www.fleishers.com

SPECIALTY Whole-animal butchery.

FAVORITE CUT Pig cheeks.

ABOUT Joshua and Jessica Applestone opened Fleisher's in 2004, where they practice a true "nose-to-tail" philosophy: they use every part of every animal, even making stocks and soap. They also run training programs for butchers.

## O. OTTOMANELLI & SONS PRIME MEAT MARKET

285 Bleecker St.
New York, NY 10014
(212) 675-4217
www.ottomanelli.com

SPECIALTY Prime meats, exotic wild game.

FAVORITE CUT Prime rib.

ABOUT Onofrio Ottomanelli learned his trade in the early 1930s from his paternal grandmother in Bari, in southern Italy. He later trained with his brother Joe and his uncle in the United States and eventually took his skills to Greenwich Village, where he passed on his expertise to his sons and grandson, who run the market today.

## OTTOMANELLI BROTHERS

1549 York Ave.
New York, NY 10028
(212) 772-7900
www.nycotto.com

SPECIALTY Dry-aged prime beef.

FAVORITE CUT Dry-aged prime New York strip steak.

ABOUT Since 1917, Ottomanelli Brothers has been a recognized processor, wholesaler, and purveyor of high-quality meats. Today, the shop is run by the fourth and fifth generations of the family.

## SAVENOR'S MARKET

160 Charles St.          92 Kirkland St.
Boston, MA 02114     Cambridge, MA 02138
(617) 723-6328          (617) 576-6328
www.savenorsmarket.com

SPECIALTY Prime and local beef, veal, lamb, poultry, and game.

FAVORITE CUT Prime rib.

ABOUT For more than seventy years, Savenor's Market has been a Boston landmark. During that time, the combination butcher shop and grocery has consistently carried the finest meats and produce, drawing such prominent customers over the years as the Rockefellers, the Kennedys, and America's first celebrity chef, Julia Child.

## THE MEAT HOOK

100 Frost St.
Brooklyn, NY 11211
(718) 349-5033
www.the-meathook.com

SPECIALTY Sustainably raised local meats and specialty sausages.

FAVORITE CUT "Man steak" (bone-in beef sirloin).

ABOUT Tom Mylan, Brent Young, and Ben Turely, who worked together at the popular Marlow & Daughters butcher shop, opened The Meat Hook in November 2009. They pride themselves on having the best-quality local meat at the lowest possible price served up with the friendliest service.

## UNION MEAT COMPANY

225 Seventh St. SE
Washington, D.C. 20003
(202) 547-2626
www.unionmeat.com

SPECIALTY Prime and choice Angus beef and fresh domestic lamb.

FAVORITE CUT Prime aged rib roast, New York strip steak, lollipop rib lamb chop, and loin veal chop.

ABOUT Opened in 1946 by brothers Bill and Ray Glasgow, the shop is located in the historic Eastern Market, built in 1873. The market suffered a devastating fire in 2007, but Union Meat and its fellow market merchants are thriving again in the rebuilt structure, with the second and third generations of the Glasgow family now working behind the counter.

# INDEX

# weldon**owen**

415 Jackson Street, Suite 200, San Francisco, CA 94111
Telephone: 415 291 0100  Fax: 415 291 8841
www.wopublishing.com

**THE COOK & THE BUTCHER**
Conceived and produced by Weldon Owen, Inc.
in collaboration with Williams-Sonoma, Inc.
3250 Van Ness Avenue, San Francisco, CA 94109

**A WELDON OWEN PRODUCTION**

Color separations by Embassy Graphics
Printed and bound in China by Toppan Leefung Printing Limited

First printed in 2011
10 9 8 7 6 5 4 3 2

Library of Congress Control Number: 2010942670

ISBN-13: 978-1-61628-113-7
ISBN-10: 1-61628-113-8

Weldon Owen is a division of

# BONNIER

**WILLIAMS-SONOMA, INC.**
**Founder and Vice-Chairman** Chuck Williams

**WELDON OWEN, INC.**
**CEO and President** Terry Newell
**VP, Sales and Marketing** Amy Kaneko
**Director of Finance** Mark Perrigo

**VP and Publisher** Hannah Rahill
**Associate Publisher** Amy Marr
**Editor** Julia Humes
**Assistant Editor** Becky Duffett

**Creative Director** Emma Boys
**Senior Designer** Ashley Martinez

**Production Director** Chris Hemesath
**Production Manager** Michelle Duggan
**Color Manager** Teri Bell

**Photographer** Kate Sears
**Food Stylist** Lori Powell
**Prop Stylist** Ethel Brennan
**Illustrator** Alyson Thomas

All photographs by Kate Sears except for the following: pages 78–79, Jupiterimages; pages 186–187,
Radius Images/Corbis; page 216, across from the butcher directory: Amy Aeckert (top left); David Henrich (top right);
Tami Reid (bottom left); Denise F. Milazo (bottom center right); The Original Farmers Market Los Angeles (bottom right);
front cover: Jennifer May (bottom left); Kris Davidson (bottom center)

Illustrations by Alyson Thomas on the following pages: 21, 83, 145, 191

## ACKNOWLEDGMENTS

**From Brigit Binns:** I'd like to thank the talented gang of the willing, who always seem to have time when it comes to testing or re-testing
a recipe or two: Lu Bennett, Lisa Baker Brill, Craig Goldwyn, Nancy Puccetti, Kara Thurmond, and Richard Wilson. And the tasters (aka townspeople)
of Athens, New York, who were always ready to offer their appetites and opinions on Wednesday and Saturday "Meat Nights" throughout the
summer and fall. When it comes to meat, I've been lucky enough to work with and learn from some very talented chefs. Number one is certainly
Tony Tammero, the Executive Chef at the Palm Restaurant. While I was writing the Palm cookbook, Tony taught me tricks about meat that no home
cook could have imagined. Recently, I collaborated with an inspired new voice on the carnivorous scene, Ryan Farr (see page 217). Along the way
I've also learned from greats like Jody Maroni, Jean-François Méteigner, Michael Psilakis, Hans Röckenwagner, Joachim Splichal, and of course
Craig "Meathead" Goldwyn, of AmazingRibs.com. I remain indebted to Kate Sears for her tasty photography, to Kim Laidlaw, who suggested me
for this project, to Hannah Rahill for agreeing that I was the right choice for "Meat Maven," to Amy Marr for helming the project throughout its life,
and to the unsinkable Julia Humes, who was my partner in protein day after day after day. And most of all, to my home team: Casey and Stella.

**Weldon Owen** wishes to thank the following people for their generous support in producing this book: Debbie Bondulic, Kimberly Chun,
Judith Dunham, Shane Gilman, Austin Goldin, Carol Myers, Tom Mylan, Elizabeth Parson, Karen Seriguchi, Sharon Silva, Jason Wheeler, and
Tracy White. Weldon Owen and Brigit Binns would like to extend their gratitude to the owners and workers of the butcher shops who participated
in this project: 4505 Meats, Alexander's Prime Meats and Catering, Avedano's Holly Park Market, Belmont Butchery, Bryan's Fine Foods, Clancey's
Meats and Fish, Don and Joe's Meats, Fleisher's Grass-fed & Organic Meat, Gepperth's Meat Market, Harvey's Guss Meat Co., Inc., Laurelhurst
Market, Lindy and Grundy's Meats, Marczyk Fine Foods, Nelson's Meat Market, Inc., O. Ottomanelli and Sons Prime Meat Market, Ottomanelli
Brothers, Savenor's Market, The Meat Hook, The Meat Shop, Union Meat Company, Zier's Prime Meats and Poultry.